HISTORY OF THE NASHOBAH PRAYING INDIANS

DOINGS, SUFFERINGS, SURVIVAL, AND TRIUMPH

DANIEL V BOUDILLION

History of the Nashobah Praying Indians
Doings, Sufferings, Survival, and Triumph

Book 1: Doings and Sufferings 1654-1736
By Daniel V. Boudillion

Littleton MA, 01460

PRINT ISBN 979-8-218-10320-0

Copyright © 2012, 2018, 2019, 2020, 2022, 2023

All rights reserved.

No part of this book may be reproduced in any form or by any electronic or mechanical means, including information storage and retrieval systems, without written permission from the author, except for the use of brief quotations in a book review.

RAVEN HOUSE PUBLISHING

This book is dedicated to Chief Caring Hands of the Nashobah-Natick-Ponkapoag Praying Indians, her daughter Tamara Quiet Storm, Chief's brother and head warrior Strong Bear Medicine, and to all the Massachusett Praying Indians—thank you for your friendship, brotherhood, and trust.

"For the price of a pumpkin…"

CONTENTS

Foreword	vii
1. Nashobah Plantation	1
2. Tom Dublet and Deer Island	38
3. Sarah Doublet's Indian New Town	112
4. The Last Indian	138
Afterword	163
Message From Chief Caring Hands	167
Appendix	169
Bibliography	173
About the Author	181

FOREWORD
FRIENDSHIP, FORGIVENESS, AND UNITY

I have had the amazing experience of seeing the impossible become reality, to see a people seemingly faded into the earth hundreds of years ago rise up before me, whole and well. A people whose sacred places I had walked many times in contemplation of spirit and the tragedy that befell them.

The Nashobah Praying Indians are a spiritual people. They see the world through the lens of spirit, and spirit speaks to them. They do not live random lives; they feel that what happens in the world is what is meant to happen. For them, spirit reaches out of the past and into the present and events that occurred long, long ago can find their way to come full circle in today's world, and bring healing and blessings with them.

I have gone on many medicine walks with Strong Bear Medicine and Quiet Storm—brother and daughter of Chief Caring Hands of the Nashobah-Natick-Ponkapoag Praying Indians—on their ancestral lands (and lands sacred to the Massachusett) and listened to them talk from the heart about the ancestors, medicine, spirit, and Creator. We have watched hawks and listened to owls. We have touched the earth and let smoke rise to the sky. And along the way we have become as brothers and sisters, as it should be.

But looming over the spirit of the Nashobah, and many Natives, are the tragic events of King Philip's War.

There is a place on the outskirts of Nashobah where women and children of the family of Strong Bear Medicine and Quiet Storm were slain by Colonials in 1676, and there is a place farther south where women and children of my own family were slain by Indians in the same war.

That our paths have crossed; that there is deep friendship between Strong Bear Medicine, Quiet Storm, and me, has deeper meaning and spirit-purpose when seen with spiritual eyes.

How strange and wonderful it is that we have both suffered the same familial loss and wounds, though on opposing sides, yet stand together in friendship and brotherhood today. I am reminded of Psalm 133:1, *How good and pleasant it is for brethren to dwell together in unity.*

It is a friendship that heals old wounds. Chief Caring Hands teaches from Father that what we pray for one, we pray for all. What heals the one, heals the all. So from this small kernel of brotherhood and healing I pray larger communal wounds are healed, and larger brotherhoods are formed.

Indeed, it is unity between peoples, under Creator, where our paths should lead. Recently, Quiet Storm announced plans for the first powwow in Littleton-Nashobah in more than 300 years: the Strawberry Moon Unity Powwow.

Unity.

FOREWORD

Unity between peoples. Unity between the people of Littleton today and the Nashobah whose ancestral land this is.

In 1654 the Nashobah under Chief Tahattawan, with the assistance of the Rev. John Eliot, converted to Christianity and formed the Praying Indian Planation of Nashobah, which is now Littleton. They sought unity with their English brethren, but the events of King Philip's War betrayed them.

We stand 369 years later—the Nashobah are still Praying Indians and hold church services, and through all the trials and tribulations they still hold open the hand of friendship and brotherhood.

The world has come full circle in Littleton-Nashobah. Creator has wrought miracles, and the owls hoot in the woods again. The Nashobah are among us, bright with spirit—let us meet them with open hands, and in healing and brotherhood, as was always meant to be.

A'ho!

CHAPTER 1
NASHOBAH PLANTATION

THE TOWN OF LITTLETON WAS FIRST INCORPORATED IN 1714 AS AN English township by an Act of the Great and General Court of the Province of Massachusetts Bay on November 2, under the name of Nashoba, and was renamed under its current name a year later on December 3, 1715. But for the previous sixty years Littleton had been a court-granted Praying Indian village named Nashobah Plantation, and this is where the Praying Indian story begins.

The Praying Indian era in Nashobah spanned from 1654 to 1736, when the last Indian, an elderly lady named Sarah Doublet, passed away, deeding her lands to her caretakers. If you have ever taken a walk in the Sarah Doublet Forest, located on the rocky hill between Nagog Pond and Fort Pond, you have been to the heart of the old Indian plantation and the site of the village, and the oldest and longest-occupied Indian lands in the area. This was the location of the village, the orchards, the burial grounds, and the fort to protect the Praying Indians from the Mohawks who raided the area.

Note 1: When referring to the Praying Indian village and its Native people I use the original spelling of Nashobah, unless in the context of Old Tahattawan, where I use his pronunciation of Nashope. The more familiar Nashoba spelling is of colonial derivation.

Apostle to the Indians

John Eliot became known as the "Apostle to the Indians" due to his efforts to evangelize the local Massachusett and Nipmuck Indians. He was born in 1604 in Widford, Hertfordshire, England. Eliot aspired to the ministry, but like many religious nonconformists, he fled England to escape the persecutions of Archbishop Laud. He arrived in Boston on November 3, 1631, a young man of 27; his betrothed followed him a year later. The subsequent year he became Puritan minister and teaching Elder of the First Church of Roxbury, a post he held for nearly 60 years.

His ministry to the Indians did not begin until 1646. Previously Eliot studied the Algonquin language and formed the conviction that the "Indians were descendants of the lost tribes of Israel," according to Herbert Harwood in the *Proceedings of the Littleton Historical Society* (1896), which was a popular belief of the era. Some believe although he was sincere in his efforts, his ministry was used by political forces, according to Dr. William P. Marchione in *John Eliot and Nonantum*, published in the Allston-Brighton Tab in July of 1998.

Note 2: Eliot initially believed that the Algonquin language would show some relationship to Hebrew. However, this did not prove to be the case.

The Massachusetts Bay Colony Charter of 1629 stipulated that one of its principal goals was to spread Christianity to the Native population: "whereby our said People, Inhabitants there, may be so religiously, peaceably, and civilly governed, as their good Life and orderly Conversation, may win and incite the Natives of Country, to the Knowledge and Obedience of the only true God and Savior of Mankind, and the Christian Faith, which in our Royall Intension, and the Adventurers free Profession, is the principal End of this Plantation."

Little had actually been done to minister to the Indians, but with the deposition of King Charles in 1649 and the rise of the pro-Puritan Cromwellian parliament, there was concern among the leadership of Bay Colony that Oliver Cromwell would revoke the Charter if missionary efforts were not made. But a more immediate issue was to "civilize" the Indians and assimilate them into English culture.

It was at this juncture that Eliot's work became of considerable interest to the leadership of Massachusetts Bay, and it was the climate in which he "labored for the Indians" in the years to come.

Eliot made his first outreach to the Indians in the summer of 1646. His initial missionary effort was to the Indians at Neponset in Dorchester, who were under the Sachem Cutshamekin. This quickly ended in failure—not only did the elderly Cutshamekin reject Eliot's proselytizing; but his braves also openly ridiculed and heckled him, according to Samuel G. Drake in his *Book of the Indians*, 1845.

Note 3: Sachem is pronounced "say'-kem." Nelson's New Dictionary of the English Language, Pronouncing and Etymological, 1922. It is a term for a chief, particular to the Algonquin speaking tribes of the North Atlantic coast.

Eliot now sought a more receptive Indian leader. He was directed by the Bay Colony magistrates to Waban, the son-in-law of old Tahattawan, the sachem of Concord, according to Marchione. This proved to be a better choice than the wary Cutshamekin, and Eliot sized Waban up to be "one who gives more grounded hope of serious respect for the things of God, than any as yet I have known of that forlorn generation."

Note 4: Eliot's preferred method of oration was from atop large boulders, several of which "Eliot's Pulpits" are still to be seen. One well-known Eliot's Pulpit is in Roxbury, and there are at least two such pulpits in the Nashoba area, one in Boxborough and the other in Harvard. The Boxborough pulpit was near the junction of Route 111 and Route 495 overlooking the highway, but it was torn down about 30 years ago to build an office building. It was a perched rock, and is pictured in the book Manitou (1989) by Mavor and Dix. The Harvard Eliot's Pulpit is a collection of three huge boulders, one of which has spalling that resembles three seats. This location is thought to be a Native council place and is near other Native sacred sites. It is easy to imagine Eliot choosing significant Native council places to preach from.

Waban was indeed a good choice. He was friendly with the English and had previously moved his extended family from Concord in the early 1630s to Nonantum Hill (Newton) to be closer to the English and their settlements.

When Eliot first preached at Nonantum, he did not go there alone. With him were Thomas Shepard, Minister of Cambridge; John Wilson, Minister of Boston; and Daniel Gookin, soon to be Supervisor of Indian towns for the Massachusetts Bay Colony, as related by Marchione.

Eliot delivered his first sermon to Waban's family on October 18, 1646. It was three hours long, and much of it was delivered in the Algonquin tongue. Waban was so amenable to the Christian message that Eliot quickly moved to set him and his family up in a township of their own as Christian Indians. Only seventeen days later, the General Court had voted land for a Christian Indian village for Waban and his family.

These fast-paced events reveal several points. First, Waban had been well-selected as the initial convert. Second, that these powerful and influential Puritan ministers accompanied Eliot as observers shows the high level of interest the Puritan leadership had in this undertaking. Third, the speed of which the General Court acted to create a Praying Indian village shows not only the priority it had, but also that there was probably already a plan in place to create such villages. This was not a surprise to them; rather it was the results of a plan already in place. Last, that the man who was to oversee these villages just happened to be along was no coincidence; he was there because they were planning to do this, and he had been previously chosen to oversee it.

In the Nonantum mission we see the shadows moving behind the scenes: the highest level ministerial support, the government support, and the signs of a previously prepared plan being put into action.

When Waban asked Eliot what the name of the new town should be, Eliot responded that it should be called Nonantum, a Natick word meaning "I rejoice." Eliot supposedly went on to elaborate that the Indians "hearing the word, and seeking to know God, the English did rejoice at it."

Marchione further tells us how the Reverend Hosmer described the new Praying Indian town of Nonantum: "Mr. Eliot...furnished them, by the public aid, with shovels, spades, mattocks, and iron crows, and stimulated the most industrious with money ... The houses of the meanest were found to be equal to those of the sachems or chiefs in other places. They surrounded the town with ditches...and with a stone-wall. The Indians, thus settled, were instructed in husbandry, and were excited to a prudent as well as industrious management of their affairs. Some of them were taught such trades as were most necessary for them, so that they completely built a house for public worship, 50 feet in length and 25 feet in breadth."

Although the Nonantum experiment was meeting its objectives, it ran into hostility from the local English settlers who were not only distrustful of the Indians, but also sought their land. As a result, the entire Nonantum colony was moved to a more secluded 3,000-acre site called Natick in 1651. This is now the town of Natick, Massachusetts.

The Praying Indian Plan

The effort to evangelize the Indians was essentially a plan to Anglicize them. It was a noted saying of Eliot's that "the Indians must be civilized as well as, if not in order to their being, Christianized." (Thomas Hutchinson, *History of Massachusetts*, 1795)

But this was more than just one man's saying—it was Bay Colony policy. In November of 1644, the county courts were ordered "to take care of the Indians residing within their several shires, to have them civilized, and to take order from time to time to have them instructed in the knowledge of God." (Lemuel Shattuck, *The History of the Town of Concord*, 1835)

This attitude of Christian-equals-English is made more explicit by Lord Henry Cromwell, son of Oliver Cromwell, who in 1654 ordered 1,000 young Irish boys kidnapped and sold as slaves to the Barbados: "We could well spare them ... and they might be of use to you; and who knows but it might be a means to make then Englishmen – I mean, Christians?" (*The Cromwellian Settlement of Ireland*, by John Prendergast, 1870)

Since Massachusetts Bay Colony was an actual Puritan theocracy, Puritan Christianity was a very *English* Christianity. There was no separation of Church and State, and "Puritan" and "English" were essentially the same thing.

In Eliot's opinion at least, his Anglicizing plan had within it a certain internal logic. But the rapidity with which the Court moved to grant lands for the Christianized Natives of Nonantum also indicates that facilitating the Anglicization of the Indians was more than a religious matter, and had become a matter of State policy and priority. For one thing, the Indians were much easier to control in fixed English-underwritten villages than when they were living nomadically in the woods under their own leadership.

A key to the Christianization or Anglicization of the Indians was to place them in English-style villages. Here they were to live in English houses, wear English clothes, worship in an English meetinghouse, farm like Englishmen, and adopt English names and customs. They were to be transformed into Englishmen. Further, it was a means of segregating and controlling the Indians. The more Indians that could be persuaded to join these villages, the less threat they were to English interests. Free-roaming Indians in the woods were perceived as a threat to settled English life.

Note 5: Native names were difficult for the English to pronounce, and they often used the expedient of dubbing local Indians with English names. Occasionally these names also reflected an aspect of the bearer, such as James-the-Printer and Tom Dublet. Intentionally or not, it was part of the Anglicization process.

One method used to Anglicize Christian Indian behavior was

a set of codes of conduct. Rule-breakers were subject from two- to twenty-shilling fines, or corporal punishment. The rules adopted at Natick, the first Praying Indian village, give insight not only into Indian culture but also into what the Puritans found most offensive in Indian culture. For instance, rules were set up against idleness, premarital sex, wife beating, naked breasts, and women wearing their hair loose, or long hair on men, as outlined by Drake in his *Book of the Indians*.

The adoption of English customs and dress was partial at best, and was to some extent a blend of cultural elements. But the question of why some Indians gave up their sovereignty, and went along with the conversion process, needs to be examined. On the surface this was against their best interests.

Similar to the way that Eliot seems to have been sincere, but with complex machinations moving in the shadows behind him, there were sincere converts to Christianity and English culture; but likewise, their motivations were probably as complex.

There were two factors at work, one more visible then the other. The first was that the Massachusett Indians had been decimated in the early part of the 17th century. They had fought a costly war with the Tarratine in 1615, which was followed by the plagues of 1620. This had catastrophically reduced their numbers by a third to nine-tenths depending on the locale, according to John V. Goff, in *Remembering the Tarratines and Nanepashemet*, Winter 2004, NEARA Journal. So reduced, they could no longer adequately defend themselves from their age-old enemies, the Mohawk, and other hostile neighboring tribes.

But by allying themselves with the English—and their guns—they had some protection. By converting, they more formally put themselves under English rule (and protection). The villages were grants from the Great and General Court, and so under the rule and protection of the English Charter, and the Crown itself.

Shattuck tells us of a Squaw Sachem in 1621 so powerful and feared that, "her enemies, the sachems of Boston and Neponset, desired protection against her, as one condition of submission to the English."

Submission was a key facet of Indian-English relations, and the word comes up again and again. For example, at a General Court held at Boston on May 6, 1646, regarding a plantation that John Winthrop Jr. had begun in Pequot territory, we read that the Indians were to be relocated across a river "which may be to the good liking and satisfaction of the said Indians, and likewise to such of the Pequot Indians as shall desire to live there, *submitting* themselves to the English government, &c."

Shattuck further records that "two sachems near Wachusett, made a formal *submission* to the English government on the 8th of March 1644, and put themselves and their subjects under its protection." He also says that "Passaconaway, sachem at Merrimack and his sons, on the 20th of the succeeding June, *submitted* in like manner."

Only a minority of the Indians in New England joined the Praying Indian villages, but those who did were of the weakened tribes, primarily the Massachuset. The more powerful tribes were not interested in Eliot's proselytizing, nor did they need English protection. Only when a tribe became weakened did they become involved with Eliot's ministry.

An example is the powerful Pennacook confederacy created by Passaconaway. Passaconaway had been forced to "submit" to the English to get his eldest son out of jail, but he still remained powerful and was resistant to Eliot's proselytizing, as were his sons. But this changed after the Pennacook were decimated by the Mohawk war of 1666-1670. His son Wonalancet, who was now Sachem, had become unable to protect his tribe and opened the door to Eliot's ministry.

Another less visible motivation was the loss of the ancestral religious and spiritual sites, which were being subsumed by the English for agricultural purposes. By setting these lands aside as Praying Indian villages, the Indians were able to preserve these sites.

Support From London

Support for the Praying Indian experiment was funded from London by the Honorable Corporation for the Propagation of the Gospel in New England, more commonly known as the New England Company. The Company was formed in 1649 by an Act of British Parliament and was authorized to solicit funds for the evangelical work. According to Harwood, a "considerable sum was collected"—more than £12,000—and as of 1662 Eliot was receiving a yearly salary of £50, as related by George Madison Bodge, *Soldiers in King Philip's War*, 1906.

With this support, Eliot began printing the scriptures in the Massachuset N-dialect of the Algonquin language, which he learned from the Massachuset Natick Indians. In 1654 he printed a Catechism, followed by Genesis in 1655. His translation of the Psalms came out in 1658. The New Testament was finished in 1661, and the entire Bible, the *Mamusse Wunneetupanatamwe Up-Biblum God* ("The Massachuset Bible") came out in 1663. These were some of the very first books printed in New England.

Oliver Cromwell was a member of the Parliament that created the New England Company. If there was any worry in the next few years when he came to power that he might revoke the charter over lack of missionary work, the existence of the New England Company should have allayed these fears. Rather, the Christianizing was less of a charter issue and more of a control and Anglicization policy towards the Indians.

The New England Company is still in existence today, and it continues its evangelizing among Native peoples.

Note 6: From the New England Company website: "The New England Company can lay claim to being the oldest missionary society still active in Britain. It was founded by an Act of Oliver Cromwell's Parliament on 27 July 1649. Following the restoration of the monarchy it was granted a Royal Charter by Charles II in 1662. The Charter provided for the promotion and propagation of 'the Gospel of Christ unto and amongst the heathen natives in or near New England and parts adjacent in America'. To this end the Company sent both missionaries and teachers to New England and later further afield to Virginia and New York. The administration was undertaken by a group of Commissioners appointed by the Company who were prominent local citizens; normally the Governor of Massachusetts was the chairman. Although early efforts were made to teach and evangelise in local languages, recruitment difficulties compelled the Company more and more to undertake the work in English, by persuading the native people to settle in one place and attend school."

Praying Indian Villages

From the years 1646 to 1675, Eliot worked to set up what eventually became 14 such Christian Indian plantations, which were more commonly called Praying Indian villages. The first seven were called the Old Villages and were considered the most loyal to the English, and were primarily the Massachusett; the last seven, mostly Nipmuck, were called the New Villages and had not established as strong a loyalty by 1675 when the Indian war called King Philip's War broke out. The villages were (in the order established):

Old Villages: Natick (Natick), Punkapoag (Canton), Hassanamesit (Grafton), Okommakamesit (Marlborough), Wamesit (Chelmsford-Lowell), Nashobah (Littleton), and Makunkokoag (Hopkinton-Ashland)

New Villages: Manchage (Sutton), Chabanakongkomun (Webster-Thompson), Maanexit (Fabyan, Thompson, Connecticut), Quantisset (southeast Woodstock and southwest Thompson, Connecticut), Wabaquissit (southwest Woodstock, Connecticut), Pakachoog (Worcester-Auburn), and Waeuntug (Uxbridge)

Note 7: According to the Supervisor of Indian towns, Daniel Gookin, there were also two other villages in Nipmuck country that were in a formation stage: "There are two other Indian towns, viz. Weshakim [Sterling] and Quabaug [SE Brookfield], which are coming on to receive the gospel: and reckoning these, there are nine in the Nipmuck country. But they being not fully settled, I omit them."

From Daniel Gookin's *Historical Collections of the Indians in New England*, 1674, we know the total population of the 14 villages was about 1060 Indians. This works out to about 75 people per village on average, with about 15 families per village on average.

The first successful conversions were among Waban's people in Nonantum, but Waban himself was from Concord and had married Tasunsquaw, the eldest daughter of the Concord sachem Old Tahattawan. It was to these Concord Indians that Eliot preached as well early on, and we read in Drake that in the autumn of 1646 that "another company of Praying Indians was established at Concord." This company was not an established Praying village, but a group of Indians who resided in the general area and had religious meetings under Eliot's guidance.

To this company of Indians a much longer list of rules—29 in all—was formed by Capt. Simon Willard, and "agreed upon by divers Sachems and other principle men," according to Shattuck. These rules seemed less geared toward prevailing Indian culture and were more or less an elaboration of the Ten Commandments. The rules specifically against Indian cultural motifs included no powwowing (shamanism), no greasing, and no "howling" at funerals. As in Natick, transgressing the rules was subject to fines or corporal punishment.

Note 8: Greasing was the Indian practice of smearing themselves with bears' grease to ward off mosquitoes. This was effective, but for some reason the English did not like the habit and proscribed against it. Provisions against it are often seen with provisions against powwowing, and there seems to have been some connection between the two that is no longer clear. Perhaps greasing in some instances was done with concoctions similar to European "witches' ointments," which are thought to have had hallucinogenic qualities.

Eliot continued to proselytize in Concord and elsewhere, and over the next seven years set up four more Praying Indian villages. The management of Praying villages combined elements of both English town governance with biblical governance. According to Alfred Sereno Hudson in *The History of Concord Massachusetts*, 1904, Eliot had them "adopt the government that Jethro proposed to Moses in the wilderness, whereby they were to choose rulers of hundreds and fifties and tens."

The Praying villages were in other ways quite similar to an English governance system. The adult male population elected their own local leaders and drafted legislation. But these village laws had to be approved by the Supervisor of Indian Towns, Daniel Gookin. They also had regular town officials such as constables, for instance.

For the most part the leaders of the New Villages were the local sachems who had converted. But as these original hereditary leaders died out, Eliot replaced them with elected or appointed leaders, thus breaking up the Native traditional leadership modes. In *Behind the Frontier* by Daniel Mandell, 1996, we read that the "Puritan missionaries labored with their native allies to develop new networks that could operate independently of aboriginal kinship and political ties."

This switching of leadership from sachems to appointments was another means of replacing Indian culture with English culture. This policy was so offensive to the stronger tribes that Uncas, for example, the Mohegan leader who was loyal to the English, "warned Eliot not to enter Mohegan territory," according to Mandell.

Cutshamekin, also no fan of Eliot, was quite clear on why he opposed the Praying Indian towns—they undermined Native authority. According to Drake, he said words to the effect of "the Indians that pray to God do not pay me tribute, as formally they did." Wonalancet, son of Passaconaway, was likewise concerned that if he converted, his people would leave him; when he did convert, those fears were realized.

The Praying Indian towns also had ministers and sent out missionaries. The first Indian church that was recognized as such by the Puritan Church as qualifying to administer sacrament was the one established in Natick in 1661.

Some of the early villages, Nonantum in particular, most likely had converts from tribes and villages all over Massachusetts Bay.

Writing in 1649 of his work in Nonantum, Eliot said: "Some Sudbury Indians, some of Concord Indians, some of Maestick [Mystic] Indians, and some of Dedham Indians, are ingenious and pray to God and sometimes come to the place where I teach and hear the word."

Waban was the leader of Nonantum, and his family were originally from Musketaquid (Concord). In 1651 Nonantum was relocated from Nonantum Hill on the Charles River in Newtown to Speen land about six to seven miles west and became the Praying Indian village of Natick, also located on the Charles. It is clear that people of several different villages were gathered here; certainly Musketaquid and Natick Indians, including the Awassamug family, and whomever had heard the word and been converted prior in Nonantum.

But the Indians mentioned in Eliot's 1649 missive and the Indians involved in Natick were of the Massachusett Federation, not a mix of neighboring peoples. The southwesterly Nipmuck had not yet come into the Praying Indian picture, although they would be the focus of the seven "New Villages." Eliot's initial conversions were of the Massachusett, and the makeup of the seven "Old Villages" reflects this.

Neighboring Makunkokoag, established between 1659 and 1660, was similar to Natick as having a mix of Massachusett peoples. Temple characterized Eliot as having here "gathered the Indians, from various quarters, into a clan here..." (J. H. Temple, *History of Framingham, Massachusetts*, 1887)

But this does not hold true in all instances. As Eliot got up steam, rather than gathering converts into new towns, he converted existing villages into Praying Indian villages. Wamesit and Nashobah are two examples. At these locations they were one people, not a gathering of peoples.

Note 9: Makunkokoag is the first Praying village where we can identify Nipmuck converts, and was closer to the Nipmuck then any village so far. There was much coming and going between the Praying villages, and as time went on and the New Villages established, we find Nipmucks involved the original southeastern Praying villages, especially Natick, which was the mother village and where Eliot preached.

Tahattawan and Concord

Old Tahattawan was a powerful sachem of the Massachusett, and like his son-in-law Waban, is said to be one the first converts to Christianity, and heard Eliot preach at Nonantum. Yet there was a considerable delay before Nashobah Praying Indian village was granted, and four other grants were made into Praying Indian villages in the interim. The issue, Harwood tells us, was "because of strong opposition on the part of some Indians." Harwood supposes the Concord Indians who were converts moved to Natick until the issue was resolved. Shattuck speaks of an early convert, Tantamouse, who like Waban and Tahattawan converted in 1646, and "embraced Christianity and removed to Natick." This would seem to support the exodus there until the issue was resolved.

Certainly, there was resistance. The Rev. Thomas Shepard of Cambridge relates such in his 1648 tract, *The Clear Sunshine of the Gospel Breaking Forth Upon the Indians of New England*: "when diverse of his [Tahattawan's] men perceived their sachem's mind, they secretly opposed him therein."

Shepard says that Tahattawan responded to this resistance with a speech. The speech as recorded is as flattering to the English as if had they written it themselves, and was the exact reverse of what the situation typically was between the English and the Indians.

According to Shepard, Tahattawan said, "The higher Indian Sachems, what did they care for you? They only sought their own ends out of you, and therefore would exact upon you, and take away your skins and your kettles & your wampum from you at their own pleasure, & this was all that they regarded; but you may evidently see that the English mind no such things, care for none of your goods, and only seek your good and welfare, and instead of taking way, are ready to give to you."

Shepard concludes this seemingly powerful endorsement of English ways with the admission that he did not actually hear the speech, but informs us it was "related by an eminent man of that town [Concord] to me."

Old Tahattawan's choice for an Indian Plantation was the lands of Nashobah, all of which is now the town of Littleton and part of Boxborough. Daniel Gookin describes Nashobah glowingly in *Historical Collections*: "the land is fertile and well stored with meadows and woods. It hath good ponds for fish adjoining it." This is echoed by the English neighbors in 1670, who report it was "exceedingly well meadowed," as recounted in 1904 by Alfred Sereno Hudson in *The History of Concord, Massachusetts*.

This was not just any old piece of ground. Eliot goes on to inform us that in actuality, "Nashope" [Nashobah] was Old Tahattawan's "chief place of residence."

. . .

What exactly the conflict was over regarding this area being turned into a Praying village is unknown. However, we do know that the Nashobah lands were not vacant lands. As mentioned by Eliot, it was where Sachem Tahattawan lived, and if he lived there, so did his extended family and many of his tribe.

Also living in Nashobah were shaman, called Powwows at the time. Tantamouse, although a convert to Christianity and an Indian minister, was also a practicing Powwow, and continued to live this dual role his entire life. According to a deposition in the *Southern Middlesex Registry of Deeds*, Vol. 9, Page 106, Tantamouse was living in Nashobah as early as 1634.

Note 10: Harwood on page 105 of the Proceedings says "it must be remembered that the oldest Indians lived in Nashobah from 1646." Indians have lived in what we call Nashobah for millennium, but what I believe Harwood is trying to say here is that some of the very first Concord converts from Eliot's preaching at Nonantum were living in Nashobah, "Praying village" or not.

All the Sachems had Powwow advisers, and it would appear that Tantamouse, the Praying Indian minister-shaman, agreed with Tahattawan that Nashobah should be a Praying Indian village. Tantamouse was not secretly a shaman among the Indians; they all knew even if the English didn't. There must have been a compelling reason Nashobah was to be reserved by deed as a village, and it seems they both wanted this to be so.

Even Eliot did not understand the desire for this place to be a Praying village. He thought it was too close and encroached on, and asked Tahattawan if he agreed. Tahattawan did agree, but said this was where the Praying village must be. (Thomas Shepard, *The Clear Sunshine of the Gospel Breaking Forth Upon the Indians of New England*, 1648)

Between the Waters

Nashobah is an Algonquin word derived from *Nashope* (pronounced Nash-o-pee). According to John C. Huden in *Indian Place Names of New England*, 1962, it means "between waters." The root *"nash"* means a "place between" or "in the middle," as defined by William Wallace Tooker in the September 1897 issue of the *American Anthropologist*. The suffix –pe is from *nippe*, meaning "water"' (James Trumbull, Natick Dictionary, 1903), and is used the same way as the –pee in Chicopee, which means moving or turbulent water.

Trumbull translates "between" as *Nashaue*, and Tooker points out that the Penobscot word "nātuah" is of the same derivation, the t being interchangeable with s throughout the Algonquin speaking regions. The Nipmuck dialect is very similar to the Massachusett-Natick, and the Nipmuck Association of Connecticut *Historical Series Number 3*, 1995, concurs that Nashoba means "the place between," or "between waters."

These waters were moving or turbulent, denoting rivers. As such, *Nashope* originally comprised the area between the Nashua, Merrimack, Concord, and Assabet rivers. Were *Nashope* meant to denote a place between non-moving waters—ponds—it would have been pronounced something akin to "Nashopaug."

Nashope later became Nashobah and then Nashoba, but phonetic spellings resonant of the original pronunciation survived as Nashobey and Neshobe, as will be discussed later.

While many have thought that Nashobah means "double ponds" or "double waters," it's inaccurate. This is a misread that came from correspondence between Herbert Harwood and John Currier in 1885 and published in the *Proceedings of the Littleton*

Historical Society in 1896. In these letters, Currier, who is seeking information on the name Neshobe, misreads the meaning as "double ponds," and this has been repeated ever since, even though in the third of the letters published, he realizes his mistake. Currier comes to the conclusion that the name should really have something to do with "between" and "half-way." In this he is correct about the root "nash" and understands the suffix has to do with water, but stumbles again when he tries to put it together as "half-way pond" or "water between other ponds." The correct suffix for pond is –*paug* and its derivatives, as will be discussed further about Nagog Pond.

Note 11: John Currier contacted Harwood over a similarity of place-names. Specifically, he wrote Harwood about the name of an Indian character in Daniel Thompson's 1839 Green Mountain Boys named Neshobee, and connects the story to Captain Josiah Powers who settled the new town of Neshobe, Vermont (now the town of Brandon). Currier links Neshobee to the town of Neshobe, and Neshobe to Nashobah via the Powers clan. However this may be, Huden says "Neshobe" is a Natick word in its own right that means "very full of water."

Note 12: In a bizarre twist on the name game, Currier in his 1914 book How Neshobe Came Up Into the Green Mountains calls Nashoba "double water, or a locality where there are two ponds, or bodies of water, spectacle shaped." He cites as his authority the Proceedings of the Littleton Historical Society, pages 117-121, of which is in actuality the published letters of his own faulty work, and his final letter correcting his work. Yet, in his 1914 volume, he not only falls back to the faulty work, and ignores his corrective, but references both (and himself) as the authority for his etymology.

Although it has no immediate bearing on our study, it is interesting to note that Nashoba is the Chickasaw word for wolf. (The Chickasaw tribe is from Tennessee.)

The name Nashobah has been spelled in a variety of ways. These variations cast light on how it might have been originally pronounced. Although the Court spelled it Nashobah, and Gookin routinely used this spelling, Eliot always spelled it *Nashope*. Eliot could speak and write Algonquin and was probably the most fluent English speaker of this language in his day, so how he spelled it was certainly significant. If Eliot wrote it as *Nashope*, we can assume this is how Old Tahattawan pronounced it.

Other spellings include a 1660 agreement between the Indians of Nashobah Plantation and the town of Concord over a conflict of rights concerning the abutting Concord New Grant. This agreement spells the name Mashoba. Walter Powers' deed from the Indians in 1694 and this testament deed of 1704 both spell it as Nashoby. The 1701 deed from the Indians to Josiah Whitcomb spells it Meshouah. The 1702 petition from Powers, Whitcomb, Bulkeley, and Henchman records it as Nashobey. John Currier has it as Neshobe. When the town of Littleton was incorporated in 1714, it was originally incorporated under the name Nashoba, which is the spelling we are most familiar with and use today.

Note 13: *The 1660 agreement is titled "An Agreement between the Ingenes of Mashoba and the Towne of Concord" (Ancient Records of Concord, Vol. 1, Page 160).*

Nashobah Plantation: 1654

Whatever the conflict was over the Nashobah lands being turned into a Praying Indian village, this seems to have been resolved by Tahattawan to the extent that the village was petitioned to the court as a town in 1654. Eliot had given the Indians the option of choosing where they wanted their Praying villages to be, and Tahattawan was adamant it should be in Nashope.

With the way clear to put the Concord Indians in an English-style village, Eliot petitioned the Great and General Court on May 4, 1654. The petition was granted the same year and Nashobah Plantation was established as the sixth Praying Indian village.

Nashobah can be assumed to have had at least 50 members from the beginning. We ascertain this from the Nonantum days when Eliot set up the Biblical form of governance that "Jethro proposed to Moses," where rulers were chosen of hundreds, fifties, and tens. Eliot tells us in 1670 in his *Brief Narrative* that Old Tahattawan, by then deceased, had been "a Ruler of 50 in our Civil Order."

Note 14: The full title of Eliot's Brief Narrative is A Brief Narrative of the Progress of the Gospel Amongst the Indians in New England, In the Year 1670: A letter to the Commissioners for the Propagation of the Gospel. The letter was written to the commissioners of the Honorable Corporation for the Propagation of the Gospel in New England, more commonly known as the New England Company.

The numbers in Nashobah never seem to have wavered much from this, and it was consistently one of the smallest Praying Indian villages. In 1674, Daniel Gookin records a population of 50 in his *Historical Collection of the Indians*, as compared to the average of 75 per village that can be extrapolated from his figures at this time. The following year John Hoar of Concord, who was sheltering the Nashobah during King Philip's War, counted them at fifty-eight of "all sorts," as Hudson puts it.

The Massachusett Federation

We first meet the Massachusett as a powerful federation of peoples under one or two Grand Sagamores of the royal family, with a hierarchy of sub-sachems under tribute or alliance with them. Although the general territory of the Massachusett is easy enough understood, it was to some extent fluid, based on the ebb and flow of alliances, wars, successions, and epidemics. As the power and numbers of the Massachusett decreased, so too did their territories and tributaries. As such, the Massachusett held sway over a territory that fluctuated from the Contact era to King Philip's War, as fortunes waxed and waned.

Nashobah Plantation was situated within the western extent of the once-powerful Massachusett Federation's territory, which prior to the English had encompassed a good 90 miles of coast and extended well inland.

Massachusetts Bay and Plymouth Colonies roughly comprised the original lands of the Massachusett Federation, or generally what are now the counties of Essex, Middlesex, Suffolk, and Norfolk, and a good part of Plymouth, based on a composite of sources. One particularly good source is the map of Massachusett Federation villages circa 1620 published online by the Massachusett Tribe at Ponkapoag.

The Massachusett Federation was governed and held under several powerful sagamores and their allies, in particular Grand Sagamore Nanepashemet and Sagamore Chickataubut, to whom a number of lesser Sachems paid tribute. Nanepashemet's seat was Pawtucket (Lynn), and his territory is said to have extended from the Piscataqua River (Portsmouth, New Hampshire) south to the Charles River, and westerly to at least Musketaquid (Concord). (Website, *The Massachusett Tribe at Ponkapoag*, 2019)

According to Gookin, Nanepashemet could "arm for war about 3000 men." As part of his defenses against the Tarratine,

Nanepashemet established imposing castle-like forts on the North Shore in Salem and Ipswich, both of which are still remembered by the name of Castle Hill. Two similar forts were said to have been in Marblehead, and another two reported in Medford.

Chickataubut apparently held from the Charles River south, from Neponsett (Dorchester) to Pawtuxent (Plymouth) and westerly towards the Worcester area. (Website, *The Massachusett Tribe at Ponkapoag*, 2019)

As attested in 1650 by Webcowit, who had married Nanepashemet's widow Squaw Sachem, Chickataubut's territory extended from his principal village at Titicut (Lakeville/Middleboro), up through Nishamagoquanett (Duxbury), northerly through his other principal village at Passonagesit (Weymouth), and then to Wanamampuke (head of the Charles River). From Titicut his territory extended westerly to Nunckatatescett (Bridgewater) and, it is thought, well beyond.

Note 15: "Pecunke, Ahivmpum, Catacimah, Webacowett, and Masbanomett doe all afferme, that Chickatawbutt his bounds did extend from Nishamagoquanett, near Duxbury mill, to Teghtacutt, neare Taunton, and to Nunckatatescett, and from thence in a straight linne Wanamampuke, which is the head of the Charles Riuer; this they doe all sollomly afferme, saing, God knoweth it to bee true, and knoweth theire harts. Dated the fires to the fourth month, 1650. Witness: Encrease Nowell, John Eliot, John Hoare." (John Eliot is the Rev. John Eliot, and John Hoare is the Concord lawyer that figures prominently as a friend of the Nashobah Indians.) (Records of the Colony of New Plymouth of New England, Vol. I., 1633-1640)

There is reason to believe that Nanepashemet and Chickataubut were brothers.

After Nanepashemet's death, Chickataubut became the Grand Sagamore of the Massachusett, and his territory and influence expanded northerly into Nanepashemet's old holdings, with some indications suggesting as far north as the Merrimack River. The Braintree Historical Society reports that he "ruled lands from Merrimack to the north, to the Charles to the west, and to the Narragansetts on the Rhode island boundary."

Like Nanepashemet, Chickataubut had once commanded about 3,000 men. But in 1633 he fell victim to an epidemic and was succeeded by his brother Cutshamekin, who was succeeded in 1660 by Chickataubut's son Wampatuck.

By 1644 Cutshamekin had grown considerably in power, holding sway over Passaconaway to the north and the Nipmuck as far west as Nashaway (Sterling/Leominster) and Quaboag (Brookfield), including the Sachems of Wachusett. (Richard W. Cogley in *John Eliot's Mission to the Indians before King Philip's War*, 1999, which cites a 1648 letter from William Pynchon to Governor Winthrop.)

Cutshamekin goes so far to as to inform Eliot in 1648 that the Quaboag and Nashaway Nipmucks were "his subjects," and were entitled to his protection. (Cogley)

Indeed, the Massachusett had long held tribute over many of the Nipmuck, and Gookin reports in 1674 that the "old men" of the Massachusett reported that "in former times" their Sachems controlled many of the Nipmucks from Nashaway to Pocumtuck (Deerfield).

Note 16: The practice of Massachusett Federation dominion over Nipmuck lands continued even up to King Philip's war, immediately before which the Sachem of the Wachusett was

Nanamocomuck, the eldest son of Passaconnoway. Nanamocomuck had reportedly once lived at Nashobah and had land there.

Nashobah: A Massachusett Federation Village

Abutting Nashobah to the southeast was Concord. It was known as Musketaquid, which according to Shattuck was "the original Indian name for Concord and Concord River" and "had been one of the principal villages of the Massachusetts tribe."

It was here that Nanepashemet's widow—known only to history as the Squaw Sachem—initially set up her seat of tribal authority after her husband was killed by the Tarratine in his fort in Mistic (Medford) in 1619.

Her choice of Musketaquid for her royal seat confirms Concord was not only a Massachusett village, but a highly important one, exactly as stated by Shattuck. According to Hudson, "Their [Musketaquid] relations were with the Mystics, whose headquarters were at Medford." Medford (Mystic/Mistic) is of course where Squaw Sachem's husband Nanepashemet had his fort and was killed.

It is also likely that Musketaquid was the Squaw Sachem's childhood village, and she had retreated there during or after the Tarratine war for safety.

Note 17: Among the Massachusett, when a sagamore died, his widow often returned to her home village.

Old Tahattawan is thought to be related to the Squaw Sachem, probably a brother. He was certainly a powerful Massachusett Sachem in his own right, a sagamore "of the [royal] blood" according to Eliot. History reveals Tahattawan to have held considerable sway as sagamore, not only in Musketaquid, but also in neighboring Nashobah as well.

Note 18: In 1684, when the Great and General Court confirmed the 1637 Indian deed to Concord, Tahattawan is referred to as "Tohuttawun Sagamore." (Middlesex Deeds, Lib. 9, fol. 105)

Indeed, Hudson flat-out states that Tahattawan (and Squaw Sachem) were "two of the aboriginal owners of the Concord Territory." They were apparently confirmed as the sole purveyors when the Great and General Court granted Concord permission on May 17, 1637, to purchase land from the "Indians, to wit, Atawans [Tahattawan] & Squa Sachim." (*Massachusetts Records*, Vol 1, Page 196)

Note 19: The transaction between Squaw Sachem and Sagamore Tahattawan, and Major Simon Willard and associates, was conducted in 1636 under an ancient oak in Concord called Jethro's Tree, near the milldam at Monument Square. It is also said that the nearby house of the Rev. Peter Bulkeley played a role in the proceedings.

Hudson also records the tradition regarding Nashawtuc Hill in Concord, "east of the river, near south bridge," that "at or near the foot of this hill is the wigwam of Tahattawan, and the squaw Sachem." This is in fact the historical site of Musketaquid village.

Hudson then adds that in a 1642 deed in which Tahattawan granted 3,760 acres [approximately six square miles] on both sides of the Concord River to Symon Willard, "Nattahatawants [Tahattawan] is referred to as 'sachem of that land' and is referred to by some writers as sachem of Musketaquid (Concord)." (Suffolk deeds Vol. No. 34) Tahattawan was a powerful ruler indeed, to be granting out this type of acreage in Musketaquid.

By 1642, Squaw Sachem had disappeared from Concord affairs. This is in all likelihood due to the fact that by 1637 she and Webcowit had moved back to the Massachusett original seat of power in Mistic (Medford/Winchester), near where her three sons Wonohaquaham, Montowampate, and Wenepoykin had set up their respective Sachemships in Mishawum (Charlestown), Abousett (Saugus River), and Naumkeag (Salem) as they came of age.

Note 20: In 1637 Squaw Sachem was deeding land in both Musketaquid and Mistic, but had reserved lifetime rights to Mistic, which indicates she was living there. This, and the fact we hear no more about her in Musketaquid, support the notion that she had left Musketaquid by 1637, if not earlier. (Ellen Knight, The Sachems of the Massachusetts Bay, 2018)

From 1642 onward, we hear about Sagamore Tahattawan as the sole ruler of Musketaquid and Nashobah. Squaw Sachem and the Massachusett seat of power were once again in Mistic. Musketaquid had been the royal seat of the Massachusett Federation from the death of Nanepashemet in 1619, to sometime between 1629 and 1637, when Nanepashemet's sons came of age around 1629, and 1637 when Squaw Sachem, the "Queen of Mysticke," is known to have been in primary residence in Mistic.

Musketaquid and Nashobah continued on under Old Tahattawan, once again quiet inland villages, loyal to Squaw Sachem.

To the north and northeast of Nashobah were the various tribes of the powerful Pennacook confederation under Passaconaway, which were allied with the Massachusett if not a branch of the Massachusett themselves. The Nashaway were westerly, and to the southwesterly was Nipmuck territory.

The Nashobah Indians have in modern times been inaccurately identified as Nipmuck, and John Swanton in his *Indian Tribes of North America*, 1953, incorrectly lists Nashobah as a Nipmuck village. Some members of the modern Nipmuc Nation feel that Nashobah also had a Pennacook presence, but if so, the Pennacook were still a Massachusett branch or allied to them. Most significantly, Old Tahattawan was a Sagamore of the Massachusett royal line that had its seat in neighboring Musketaquid, and "Nashope" was his primary residence.

Nashobah could only have been a Massachusett village.

Note 21: Following the Tarrantine wars and the plagues, the once-dominant Massachusett were decimated, and what was left were further reduced in King Philip's War in 1675 and in repeated Mohawk sniping. This left a power vacuum, particularly in the western areas of their territory. Other tribes such as the nearby inland Nipmuck, who had not been so adversely affected by the devastation wrought by the Tarrantine and plagues in the coastal areas, claimed these now reduced and vacated territories over time and well into the modern era. This is the root of the misimpression that the Nashobah were not Massachusett, but Nipmuck. But in Praying Indians times and earlier, Nashobah was Massachusett ancestral territory under Massachusett Sachems.

The Massachusett tribes still live and gather on their ancestral lands—for example, the Praying Indians of Natick and Ponkapoag (Canton) led by Naticksqw, Chief Caring Hands.

It is Chief Caring Hands' people who are most closely linked to Nashobah.

Bounds of the Old Plantation

The bounds of Nashobah Plantation were an artificial construct of straight lines drawn into a square on paper and meant to define a wilderness area of hills, lakes, woods, and meadows into a sixteen-square-miles tract. Where exactly the English and Indians thought this square actually fell on the ground in 1654 is unknown, except in the most general terms.

For one thing, we don't see the Plantation being actually laid out until Eliot petitioned the Court in 1659 for Jonathan Danforth to lay out Nashobah on the ground as well as other Praying Indian villages. The original document, in John Eliot's script, can be found in the *Massachusetts Archives*, Vol. 30, Page 81. Also, if there was ever any question about how Eliot spelled Nashobah, this document, written in his own hand, shows him spelling it *Nashope*. Although there were several surveys by Danforth of Nashobah over the years, I have not been able to find a copy of the survey plan petitioned by Eliot in 1659.

Note 22: *The date on Eliot's petition is difficult to decipher, it appears to read "this 21 of the 8th 59," which would seemingly be the 21st day of the 8th month of 1659: Aug. 21, 1659. But the index renders it as Oct. 21, 1659. I believe Eliot is recording the date in the Julian calendar (Old Style), in which case it should be rendered into the New Style Gregorian as <u>Nov.</u> 21, 1659. The Oct. vs. Nov. index discrepancy is, I believe, a scrivener's error in rendering the Old Style date into the New Style calendar.*

(The modern online index references the Oct. 21, 1659 date, but gives the document itself a date of "1660-05-31," which is nowhere to be found on the document itself.)

Note 23: *Also included in Eliot's 1659 petition is the request that the Praying Indians not be allowed power to sell Indian Plantation lands. This was to prevent unscrupulous land dealers* *from acquiring the plantations out from under the Indians and rendering them indigent.*

The initial survey, when it was done, was an inaccurate walk through the woods at best, where trees were blazed along the way in wandering lines, far from straight; for example, the northerly line, which was supposed to have been four miles long, was laid out as three miles. As well, the lengths were more to the distance of five miles then the stated four.

But at least after the trees were blazed, people had a better idea of what was supposed to be the plantation than before. Before the first Danforth plan, when the town of Concord was laying out the new grants they received from the court in what is now Acton, there was an argument in 1660 with the Nashobah Praying Indians over who had rights to part of those lands—that is, the Nashobah felt that the Concord New Grants had cut into the Plantation. This was resolved by Lieutenant Joseph Wheeler paying the Nashobah £15 in consideration for the lands in dispute. This is most likely why Eliot petitioned the court to have the Plantation surveyed by Danforth. Once laid out on the ground, this would hopefully prevent further disputes.

From this incident with the Concord New Grants, we learn that back then the easterly portion of the plantation was thought by the Indians to extend further east then we think of it today. To give a rough estimate of the size, the four corners after the 1660 incident with Concord are:

1. the southwest corner of Nagog Pond;
2. midpoint on the southern shore of Forge Pond;
3. the Littleton-Ayer town line on Route 2A;
4. the hill just south of the junction of Depot Road and Middle Street in Boxborough.

The Praying Indian Village

The Indian village itself was most likely in the fields and hillside at the north end of Fort Pond. There are several indicators for this. First, Fort Pond is named after the Indian fort the Nashobah Praying Indians built there near the top of the hill to protect from the Mohawk raids. This had to be close to the village to be of any use. Another indicator is that Nashobah, when meaning "between waters," is thought to refer to Nagog Pond and Fort Pond. This places the village between Nagog and Fort Pond. It would also indicate that this is where Tahattawan's "primary residence" was.

A final clue is that the Indians, after they had sold off the entire plantation some years later, were offered back a small tract for their residence. The area they chose was this area between Fort Pond and Nagog Pond, which we can deduce was the village site. The north end of Fort Pond was known as Speen's End, after a prominent Praying Indian minister who lived there in later years.

The Algonquin word Nagog may offer us clues to the village location, as well. Huden says Nagog is a Wampanoag word that can mean "at the sandy place," or "at the corner," or even "near the path."

John Currier in *How Neshobe Came Up Into the Green Mountains*, (1914) suggests that "at the corner" is in reference to "the corner of the [Indian] town at that pond." This is true enough, but there is nothing sandy about Nagog—it is a rocky pond. And unlike the murky Fort Pond, Nagog has remarkably clear waters and is fed by powerful springs as deep as fifty feet beneath the surface.

Note 24: *The town of Concord took notice of the clarity of the water and currently uses Nagog as a public water supply. The* *intake point of the pipe line is said to be five hundred feet behind the dam, in the cove.*

Significantly, Huden doesn't just link the word Nagog with the pond, but gives the full listing as "Nagog Pond and Village, Middlesex County." This locates the Indian village in the very near vicinity of Nagog Pond. Speen's End and its environs are essentially between Nagog Pond and Fort Pond, and the distance between the two lakes is only half a mile. The village was indeed between these two waters.

Although Huden has the location correct, I don't think he has it translated right. His "at the corner" transition is derived from the Wampanoag Algonquin word Nâïag, (Naquag, Naiyag): "corner."

But there is a much clearer translation: N'pog, which is an Algonquin word for "pond." Essentially, the local Indians called this body of water "the pond."

N'pog is a much closer phonetic to Nagog then Nâïag, and phonetics are important in identifying the correct Algonquin translation.

The –paug, –pog, and –bog sounding suffix in the Massachusett Algonquin means "water at rest," which is how they designated ponds. Moving water was tidal or river water. When we hear the phonetic '–og' sound at the end of a word, we know the word has something to do with a pond. (Hammond Trumbull, *The Composition of Indian Geographical Names*, 1870)

Nagog Pond

Nagog Pond is substantially different today from what it was in the time of the Indian village and Colonial era. For one thing, the pond was much lower before it was dammed by Daniel Wetherbee in 1852 to increase flowage to his mills about two miles away. According to Harold Phalen, the dam "raised the water level appreciably and produced the large island, lying wholly within the town of Littleton." There are two other areas that become islands in the spring when the water is high, but no islands existed before 1852. (*History of the Town of Acton*, 1954, Harold R. Phalen)

Early maps reflect this difference in shape. Because Nagog straddles the Littleton-Acton line, most Littleton maps only show the Littleton half of the lake, and the lake does not appear much different from this perspective. However, when paired with the corresponding Acton map, a very different portrait emerges. Compared to the other lakes in town, which still have their familiar shape, Nagog becomes peanut-shaped, with three large points of land extending into the lake, and no cove as we know it today at the dam. When the water level rose, one point of land was submerged and the other became an island. Also, it flooded across Great Road resulting in the small pond on the northeast side of the road and Great Road became a causeway.

Note 25: This unfamiliar shape can best be seen in the Henry Walling 1856 Atlas map of Middlesex County. The 1875 Beers maps of Littleton and Acton reflect this as well if you hold the maps together. The 1830 Hoar and Foster map appears to show the Littleton side of Nagog as it looks today, but without the island. This is because only half of the lake is shown, and what appears to be the spit of land on Nagog Hill Road at the Littleton-Acton line in actuality used to extend all the way out to, and include, the island.

It is also obvious from the 1875 map that the rise in the waterline was not substantial until after Concord gained the water rights and built a new dam in 1909. The 1886 USGS topo-

graphical map, Lowell quadrangle, shows a lake similar to the 1875 Atlas map, but in the 1939 Westford topographical map, the shape we know today is apparent. Based on the differences between the topographical maps, it would appear the water-level was raised ten to twelve feet since Colonial times. (Lowell Quadrangle, 1893 USGS 15-minute series, surveyed 1886; Westford Quadrangle, 1941 USGS 7.5-minute series, surveyed 1939)

Nagog Pond was also spelled Magog, but this is found mainly in Acton in the late 1800s. In the 1860 *Report of the Flowage of Meadows on the Concord and Sudbury Rivers*, which reports on the legal proceedings regarding a water-rights case, Nagog is referred to solely as "Magog." Later in 1878, when Acton stocked the pond with bass, the name is also entered as Magog in the town records.

Harold Phalen relates that "the Indian word for water is rendered in English as magog in several instances," and offers Lake Memphremagog in Vermont, meaning "beautiful water," in support of the magog spelling. (Note the -og sound at the end, as discussed above.)

At least in early times, this may reflect the English difficulty in pronouncing Indian words, especially the M and N sounds, which seemed to have been less distinct in Algonquin than in English. As related previously, Nashobah was being pronounced by the English with the M sound as well, as evidenced by both Mashoba and Meshouah, which are used in documents in 1660 and 1701 respectively.

But Nagog is spelled correctly (or *misspelled*, as the case may be) in the 1669 pasturing lease from Concord to Captain Thomas Wheeler, referring to it as "Nagog Pond."

Morning and Evening Prayers

We know very little about the Nashobah Praying Indian village other than the Indians had an orchard there, and the burial grounds were somewhere in the near vicinity.

Although the Eliot experiment required the Praying Indians to live an English-style life, instead we find a blend of cultures. Other than at Natick, the Praying Indians with very few exceptions lived in wigwams, and only in Natick were there streets laid out as such. The other Praying Indian villages were to the eye little different from any Native Indian village, other than that the fact the women were supposed to cover their breasts and the men were to wear their hair "comely as the English do," according to the rules of conduct set up in Concord. We can assume things were similar in Nashobah.

As befitting a Praying Indian village, religion played a part in everyday life. Harwood informs us in the *Proceedings* that "most of the Indians set up morning and evening prayers in the families." The Rev. James Fletcher of Acton tells us about the choir in Nashobah in his *Acton in History*, 1890. He says that "the Indians sung a psalm, made Indian by Eliot in one of our ordinary English tunes, melodiously." Fletcher is referencing a 1651 letter by "Wilson." I have not been able to find this letter though. He goes on to relate that "James Speen, with his Indian choir, sung Psalms at one of Eliot's meetings, May 14, 1654."

Note 26: Having heard the descendants of the Nashobah Praying Indians sing "Amazing Grace," I can report they have extraordinary singing voices, and sing melodiously indeed.

Note 27: I have not been able to positively identify "Wilson," but the Rev. John Wilson of the Boston Church had been involved in Eliot's ministry, and this with the 1651 date of the letter makes him a likely candidate.

We have very little insight into the daily life in Nashobah Plantation, but Eliot does record a disconcerting element about Nashope in his 1670 *Brief Narrative*. He says "Nashope is our next Praying Town, a place of much Affliction." He does not elaborate on this, but the lens of time shows that there is no happy history to any of the fourteen Praying Indian villages that Eliot created, Nashobah included.

CHAPTER 2
TOM DUBLET AND DEER ISLAND

Part 1: Before Deer Island

Brief Summary of King Philip's War: By 1675, the tension between the English colonists and the neighboring Indian tribes—in particular, the Pokanoket Wampanoag, under their Sachem Metacom, son of Massasoit—led to outright hostility. In the conflict that ensued, Metacom, known as King Philip, led an alliance of Wampanoag and Nipmuck bands against the English in New England, most particularly Bay Colony. This was a brutal no-holds-barred fight to the death, a war of survival on both sides, in which the Nashobah Praying Indians were caught in the middle.

Governance of Bay Colony

To follow the events of King Philip's War, it helps to understand the governmental structure of Massachusetts Bay Colony.

Unlike the Plymouth, Rhode Island, and Connecticut

Colonies, Massachusetts Bay had a Royal Charter from the King of England. This charter incorporated the enterprise and gave it formal legal status and the basis of its governmental legitimacy and authority. (Plymouth, for example, did not have a charter, and was based simply on Englishmen self-governing in the New World. Rhode Island and Connecticut held land patents.)

Massachusetts Bay Colony was funded by investors who held stock. Unlike other colonies, the board of directors and majority stockholders of Massachusetts Bay moved its seat of governance from London to Boston, by immigrating and buying out those who did not wish to move. This made Massachusetts Bay the first English-chartered colony whose board of directors did not live in England, but in the colony itself. This gave it considerable independence and allowed it to assert its theocratic Puritanism with little oversight from the king.

The Charter, issued in 1629, established a General Court, often referred to as the Great and General Court. It met annually to establish the laws of the colony and hear cases. In theory, all the freemen of the colony met and acted as the General Court, but in practice, the towns elected men to represent them in the General Court.

Note 1: The Charter had a number of interesting clauses, one of which was that the Crown reserved "the Fifth part of the Oar of Gold and Silver which should from time to time and at all times then after happen to be found." Apparently the "late King James the First his Heirs and Successors" had thought New England to be an Eldorado not unlike Spanish South America. It was obvious early on, though, that there was little gold and silver to be found in Bay Colony, and no one bothered to mine for it until after the Revolution. At this point, Colonials did mine for silver in the area, such as the Bromfield silver mine at Oak Hill in Harvard and the Heald mine in Pepperell.

The Heald Mine was opened in 1780 by Joseph Heald and reopened in 1880 by Daniel Bates as the Fitchburg Gold and Silver Mining Company. It is a 50-foot horizontal shaft into a hillside. No gold or silver was ever recovered. The Harvard mine was opened by Colonel Henry Bromfield in 1783 and produced a 50-foot shaft in the side of Oak Hill but little else.

There was a silver rush in the Newbury-Amesbury area from 1875 to 1878, however, in which upwards of 20 shafts were sunk and hundreds of prospecting pits and trenches dug. Little silver was recovered, but the ore contained about 50 percent lead, which paid the operational costs. (James Gage, Email correspondence with Daniel V. Boudillion, January 2020)

At its annual meeting, the General Court elected the governor, deputy governor, and 18 assistants called the Court of Assistants, or more commonly, the Governor's Council. When the General Court was not in session, the council had the power to correct, punish, pardon, govern, and rule. The assistants, called magistrates, had judicial power and heard cases.

King Philip's War

As the coming of King Philip's War clouded the horizon and the English stuck close to their garrison houses, the Praying Indians of Nashobah Plantation remained true to the English.

Note 2: The Nashobah were a band of the Massachusett Federation, an alliance of tribes and bands under Nanepashemet, and afterward his widow, Squaw Sachem. It is from the Massachusett Indians that the Commonwealth of Massachusetts is named, and was pronounced something akin to "Massachuseuk" or "Moswetuset."

Alfred Sereno Hudson in *The History of Concord, Massachusetts* in 1904 said of the Nashobah and the Praying Indians in general that "the Christian Indians stood fast in their new faith and proved firm friends of the English." They had consented to dwell in plantations (towns) like the English did, and to live and dress like the English, and to worship the English God.

They had done so even under the strain of the approaching war, knowing their alignment with the English would bring down on them the wrath of the uprising Indians, but not realizing the war would also turn the English against them as well. But for the previous 20 years at least, there had been nothing but good relations between the Praying Indians of Nashobah Plantation and their English neighbors in Concord.

This good will, however, began to wane in August of 1675, when Captain Wheeler's troops were ambushed and the English town of Quaboag Plantation (Brookfield) was besieged and burned down by Nipmuck warriors. Wolcott related in 1884 that "The Christian or 'Praying' Indians, as they were called, were suspected, probably without reason as to most of them, of sharing in the Brookfield treachery, and of sympathy with Philip [Metacom] in his general plan."

The Quaboag disaster hit close to home in both Concord and Concord Village. The ambushed troops were led by Captain Thomas Wheeler, who owned the local gristmill on Nashoba Brook, and two of the soldiers who died in the initial attack were from Concord: Samuel Smedley and Henry Young. Samuel Smedley was the brother of Mary Smedley, whose husband Isaac was killed in Concord Village by Indians in February of 1676. Captain Wheeler and his son, Lieutenant Thomas Wheeler, both died of their wounds some months later.

Note 3: James Speen, a Praying Indian of Nashobah Plantation, had also fought at Quaboag, acting as a scout and soldier for Captain Wheeler on the fateful day that Samuel Smedley died.

It would have been difficult for the men and women of Concord Village to view their Indian neighbors in Nashobah Plantation without misgivings, wondering if the rumor that Praying Indians had been involved in sacking Quaboag were true. Even the sight of an Indian would have been hard to bear for those who lost loved ones in the attack on Quaboag, even if they weren't personally responsible.

Distrust

These misgivings turned to distrust in Bay Colony as the attacks continued on English towns. Many felt insecure and at risk having the Christian Indians living among them; others viewed them with outright animosity, feeling that there were no "safe" Indians, period. There were 14 Praying Indian villages scattered throughout the Colony, and over the next three months, these English doubts turned to wariness and then to downright hostility.

As the Rev. John Eliot related on April 4, 1675, "the prophane Indians p've a sharp rod to the English, & the English p've vary sharp rod to the praying Indians." (First Church records, Roxbury)

Wolcott went on to relate that this "belief and the excitement caused by [Brookfield] induced the Colonial authorities to order the removal of the Indians of Punkapoag and the Natick to Deer Island in Boston harbor." This happened in late October 1675, the three boats leaving from the "falls of the Charles River," at midnight on the 30th. (This was the first removal of Praying

Indians to Deer Island. The Nashobah were not among them; their time of affliction was yet to come.)

Note 4: The midnight departure was due to the tide being high at that time, "the tides serving," as recounted by Gookin in his 1677, An Historical Account of the Doings and Sufferings of the Christian Indians in New England in the Years 1675-1677. *Some commentators have construed the midnight departure time in more sinister terms.*

The Praying Indians were caught in the middle. The English distrusted them and eventually interred them on Deer Island, a wooded, sandy isle in Boston Harbor. But they were distrusted by Metacom's Indians as well. Both sides thought the Praying Indian loyalties lay elsewhere, and that they were spies at best— traitors at worst.

Hudson said that although the English became everywhere distrustful of the Praying Indians, the Praying Indians nonetheless "were giving of continued loyalty, serving the Colony faithfully whenever occasion required as spies, or as allies in the ranks of the levied troops."

This is true to a good extent, yet the underlying reality was, as it often is, more complex and decidedly more human.

Praying Indian Villages

Beginning his ministry in 1646, The Rev. John Eliot became known as the "Apostle to the Indians." With the financial backing of the Honorable Corporation for the Propagation of the Gospel in New England, more commonly known as the New England Company (which was headquartered in London), he set about to translate the Geneva Bible into the Algonquin language and evangelize the Indians. He felt strongly that effective conversion could not occur without the Indians first having adopted English values and lifestyles. He then grouped his new converts into English townships, granted by the Great and General Court of Massachusetts, where they would live as English with English houses, dress, and social codes. The villages were in reality a blend of culture—a thin veneer of English custom over the deeper stratum of Indian culture. Often, the veneer went no deeper than the clothes.

The Indian township was first granted to Natick in 1651, led by Waban, who was a Concord Indian and Eliot's first convert. These Indian plantations were more commonly called "Praying Indian villages." There were 14 villages at the time of King Philip's War in 1675, broken down into two groups, the early or Old Villages, and the later New Villages

In general, the Old Villages were mostly Massachusett, and the New Villages were mostly Nipmuck. For the most part, the Old Villages stayed loyal to the English, and the New Villages sided with Metacom (King Philip), the Pokanoket sachem of the Wampanoag Confederacy.

Note 5: Metacom was the son of Massasoit, Chief Sachem of the Wampanoag Confederacy. His mother was a Nipmuck of the Quaboag band.

Major-General Daniel Gookin is another name that comes up regarding the Praying Indians. He was born in Ireland, the son of an Englishman from Kent, and immigrated to Bay Colony via Virginia when he was 32 years old. He was referred to as a Kentish soldier and was appointed the first Superintendent of the Praying Indians and worked closely with his friend Reverend Eliot on their behalf. When he moved to Bay Colony, he was a near neighbor of Eliot, thereby they became acquainted. Gookin was 63 years old at the time of King Philip's War and the Rev. Eliot was 71.

Eliot and Gookin were so associated with the Praying Indians that by the time of King Philip's War, these Indians were known as "Mr. Elliots Indians, or Captain Guggins [Gookins] Indians," according to William Hubbard in *A Narrative of the Indian Wars in New England*, 1677.

Note 6: According to A Brief History of Acton, "Guggin's Brook which enters Fort Pond in West Acton, was originally Gookin's Brook" (Acton Historical Society, 1974). Because Gookins was also spelled "Guggins" as early as 1677, I wonder if the name of the brook hasn't always been Guggins, but understood to have been named for the man better known as Gookin. Either way, Guggin's Brook is certainly associated with the Praying Indians as it has its source in Boxborough in the southeast corner of the old Nashobah Plantation. On a similar note, Heathen Meadow Brook in Stow and Acton is a tributary of Guggin's Brook.

Spies, Scouts, and Renegades

King Philip's War had a huge impact on the Praying Indians, ultimately destroying their culture, dividing their families, and reducing their numbers drastically in the process. In 1674, there were 1,100 inhabitants in 14 Praying Indian villages, who, says Shattuck in *The History of the Town of Concord*, "had ostensibly embraced Christianity. Only a part of them, however, appear to have been influenced by Christian principles." Drake, in his 1841 *Book of the Indians*, paints a more pessimistic view of their sincerity: "There is, however, not the least probability, that even one fourth of these were ever sincere believers in Christianity." How he came to this harsh determination is unexplained.

But by the fall of 1675 when the Praying Indians were being removed to Deer Island, Eliot could only tally about 500, according to Drake. This means half of the Praying Indians had either disappeared or joined with Metacom. Gookin said of them that "being raw, and lately initiated in the Christian profession, most of them fell off from the English and joined the enemy."

The choices were few and none of them good. Some Indians, like the Wamesit in Chelmsford-Lowell, wandered the wilderness, only to return cold and hungry. Those who joined Metacom faced being sold as slaves to the West Indies after the war, and those who stayed with the English were put on Deer Island. For the Praying Indians, there was nowhere safe to go, nowhere to hide. They had no one to turn to.

Drake said that King Philip's War not only shook the faith of the average Praying Indian, "but many that had been at the head of the praying towns, Indian ministers themselves, were found in arms against their white christian neighbors." Shattuck, in 1835, added that "Many of them became treacherous, and were among the worst enemies of the English."

Among these was Captain Tom (Wattasacompanum), who Gookin wrote of as "My chief assistant, ruler of the Nipmuck Indians, a grave and pious man, of the chief sachem's blood of the Nipmuck country," but who later "yielded to the enemy's arguments, and by his example drew most of the rest" of the Hassanamesit (Grafton) Praying Indians. He was later described by Edward Randolph in his report to King James II on the state of affairs in New England: "And at Natick there was a gathered church of praying Indians, who were exercised as trained bands, under officers of their owne [Captain Tom]; these have been the most barbarous and cruel enemies to the English of any others."

Note 7: There is no evidence that the Natick Praying Indians were as a whole, or in bands, or otherwise "enemies to the English." Quite the contrary, the Natick (along with the Nashobah and Punkapoag) were the most loyal of all Indians to the English in King Philip's War. How they were rewarded for this loyalty is another matter.

Another was Old Jethro (Tantamouse, also known as Aantonuish), a Massachusett who was present at the first purchase of Concord and who, embracing Christianity, moved to the Praying Indian village of Natick. In 1674, he was appointed missionary to the Nipmuck Indians at Weshakim (Sterling) but was found by Tom Dublet two years later to be sitting as a sachem in the Wachusett war camp, as well as his son Peter-Jethro of Hassanamesit, who "led a company of warriors against the Colonists" according to George F. Daniels in the 1886 *Huguenots in the Nipmuck Country.*

Then there was Mattoonus, a Nipmuck chief who as a Praying Indian lived in Pakachoog (Worcester-Auburn), and was constable of the town. According to the *Old Indian Chronicle*, he was the "principle ringleader" behind the "cruel and outrageous attempt at Quaboag [Brookfield]." Daniels says that he led the attack on Mendon "and killed four to five persons himself." He was also reportedly seen by James Quanapohit, the Praying Indian spy, taking the "lead in the war dances." He is described by Hubbard in his *A Narrative of the Indian Wars in New England* in 1677 as "an old malicious villain."

Note 8: Drake in The Aboriginal Races of North America, 1880, quotes Increase Mather: "Matoonas, who was the first Indian that treacherously shed innocent English blood in Massachusetts Colony, he some years before pretended to something of religion, being a professor in general (though never baptized nor of the in-churched Indians) that so he might the more covertly manage the hellish design of revenge that was harboured in his devilish heart."

But with few exceptions, the reality was the Massachusett Praying Indians remained loyal to the English, even under extremely trying circumstances; those who went with Metacom had typically been abused or provoked by the English.

Indeed, the Nipmuck Indians played on the fears of the Praying Indians of how the English would treat them. In Hassanamesit, just before the English arrived in November to take them to Deer Island, a party of Nipmuck warriors showed up and told them to "go with them quietly,"—that is, join them—"for if we do not kill you," the English will "force you all to some island where you will be in danger to be starved with cold and hunger, and most probably in the end be all sent out of the country for slaves." The Hassanamesit joined up, willingly for the most part. (Jill Lepore, *When Deer Island Turned Into Devil's Island*, Bostonia Magazine 2006 and George Madison Bodge *Soldiers in the King Philip's War*, 1906)

If scare tactics didn't work, the Nipmucks simply captured the Praying Indian villages, as they did in Makunkokoag, Hassanamesit, and Chabanakongkomun, as related by Bodge.

Some Praying Indians worked as spies for the English. For example, Job Kattenanit and James Quanapohit both were recruited in December 1675 from Deer Island by Major Gookin to pass among the Nipmuck and gather intelligence, which they did, alerting the English to the exact date of a planned attack on Lancaster. They had both been given the incentive of a princely five pounds each to take the job, although Job was also looking for a means off the island so he could rescue his family from the Nipmuck.

Note 9: James said of the impending attack: "And this Indian [One-eyed John, AKA Monoco] told me, they would fall upon Lancaster, Malborough, Sudbury, & Meadfeild; & that the 1st thing they would do should bee to cut down Lancaster bridge, so to hinder theire flight, & assistance coming to them; & that they intended to fall upon them in about 20 dayes time from wednesday last." (Collections of the Massachusetts Historical Society, VI. 205-208, James Quanapaug's Information.)

The information was not acted on due to English bickering, and Lancaster was attacked and burned down on the exact day that Job and James had warned it would be. Unlike attacks on other English towns, the massacre and destruction of Lancaster could have been avoided.

These were dangerous missions. James was suspected by Metacom of being a spy, and "had given out the word that certain Praying Indians should be sought after, and, if possible, seized and brought to him; for he wanted to put them to death in a cruel manner with his own hands," according to Drake. Three of these were James and Thomas Quanapohit, and James Speen.

In late February, six more Praying Indians, including Job, were recruited from Deer Island as scouts after it was learned from a young girl named Mary Powers of Concord Village, who had been abducted and escaped, that "the Indians were in three Towns beyond Quaboge."

Four of the six scouts are known to be James Quanapohit, Job Kattenanit, James Speen, and William Nahaton; the last two of which had Nashobah connections. All were described by Drake as being "six of their bravest and principle men," and Bodge added they "were greatly elated that they would now have a chance to prove their truth and worth."

There was even a company of Praying Indians that fought in the war in the earliest stages. According to Bodge and Drake, Governor Leverett ordered Major Gookin "to raise a company of Christian Indians" and "one-third of the able-bodied men in all the villages were mustered, and amounted to a company of fifty-two." Among these were James Speen of Nashobah Plantation and James and Thomas Quanapohit, all of whom served the required 25 days under Captain Isaac Johnson. These were all willing volunteers, according to Bodge, and received high praise from their officers, as did the Indian scouts.

But there was little reward for their service. Between spy jobs, Job and James were summarily reinterred on the island, and the six Indian scouts returned "utterly discouraged" by the "bitter hostility" of the English soldiers in general, according to Bodge. And those who escaped the Nipmuck for sanctuary with the English found themselves being sent to Deer Island.

No matter how sincere their efforts and intentions, there was no level of proof of loyalty from an Indian that the average Englishman would accept, despite the favorable opinion that the governor and council had of the Praying Indians. It was an overwhelming climate of fear and distrust.

Joseph Tukapewillin was the minister of Hassanamesit and the brother of its ruler Anuweekin, according to Eliot in his *Brief Narrative* in 1670. Joseph escaped the Nipmuck with his family and sought haven with the English but was instead removed to Deer Island. Before interment he was allowed to meet briefly with his old friend and teacher, the Rev. Eliot. In the face of all that had happened, he said, "I thought within myself it is better to die than to fight the church of England." But he knew he had no home with the English or elsewhere, and added, according to Gookin, "Oh Sir I am greatly distressed this day on every side; the English have taken away some of my estate, my corn, cattle, my plough, cart, chain, and other goods. The enemy Indians have also taken a part of what I had; and the wicked Indians mock and scoff at me, the English also censure me, and say I am a hypocrite. In this distress I have no where to look, but up to God in heaven to help me."

Survival was the primary issue, not loyalty, and what efforts the Praying Indians made to help the English ended badly.

For the most part, the Praying Indians who helped the English had financial or personal motivations. James got five pounds, and Job was on a personal quest to rescue his family. William's service in the Indian company kept him off Deer Island, a significant motivation. Deer Island loomed large over them all, and any job for the English was worth it to get off the island and keep off it. But we see with Job that even after rendering excellent service to the English, he was sent back to that terrible place. Joseph Tukapewillin had, as a result of his misadventures, given up all hope of God. Some historians, like Jill Lepore in *When Deer Island Was Turned Into Devil's Island*, find "undying loyalty" in his remarks to Eliot, but I read defeat and despair.

People seemed to be doing whatever they had to do to keep alive, to keep their families together, and to survive. Even the renegades had reasons for their defection. Old Jethro had suffered harsh treatment from Captain Moseley and harbored a grudge toward the English over that and a subsequent conviction for abusive and wicked speech that carried a sentence of 30 stripes with a whip. Mattoonus had a life-long grudge with the English over the execution of his son Nehemiah, and although he put on a fair face, as soon as war broke out he joined against the English. Captain Tom is more of an enigma. He was one of the Hassanamesit Praying Indians who, along with Kattenanit, Tukapewillin, and Speen, was forced by the Nipmuck to choose between them and the English. He seems to have taken that choice quite seriously, and with ruinous results, having been observed as part of the attack on Sudbury.

Trouble Draws Nigh in Chelmsford

The prejudice against the Praying Indians—for the simple fact they were Indians—had become so intense that by the end of August, the governor and his council disbanded the Praying Indian companies for their own safety. As well, all Praying Indians were confined to the five Old Villages (Natick, Nashobah, Hassanamesit, Wamesit, and Punkapoag) and were not allowed to "travel more than one mile from the center of such village except in the company of English." The council also decreed that "if any shall be found breaking these rules, the English are at liberty to shoot them down as enemies, or arrest them," as related by both Bodge and Daniels.

Note 10: I have been unable to find this document or reference to it in the Massachusetts Archives. There are similar decrees, however, but they are dated 1681 and 1704, some years after the war.

Hezekiah Ushur, a bookseller in Boston, commented at the time, (calling them *Preying* Indians) that "they have made *preys* of much English blood, but now they are all reduced to their several confinements; which is much to a general satisfaction in that respect." (Bodge, 1906)

But it was not just the English who had become vocal. On September 8, 1675, Lieutenant Thomas Henchman was ordered by the council to, among other mandates, "use your best endeavour to settle, compose & quiet matters respecting the Indians our neighbours, particularly those that hue at Wamesit, Nashobah, & Marlborough." Apparently, the council's decision had created a clamor among the Praying Indians at Nashobah and elsewhere.

The Nashobah had been living as unobtrusively as possible through these troubled months, but this did not protect them from English itchy fingers. According to Gookin's account, on November 15, 1675, 14 armed men from Chelmsford went to the nearby Praying Indian village of Wamesit (Chelmsford-Lowell). A barn of hay and corn had been burned by a passing war party, and the Chelmsford men, bent on making someone pay, sought out the Wamesit village, which had no one in it at the time but women and children.

They ordered them out of their wigwams and then fired on them without reason or warning "and wounded five women and children, and slew outright a lad of about twelve years old, which child's mother was also one of the wounded; she was a widow, her name Sarah [Wunnuhhew]," as Gookin related.

The two men whose barn was burned, Lieutenant Thomas Henchman and Lieutenant James Richardson, were friends of the Wamesit and did not believe them to be guilty. This incident simply served as an excuse for mob violence. (Lieutenant Henchman was the commander of the garrison at Chelmsford and would go on to buy half of Nashobah Plantation in 1686.)

Note 11: Two Englishmen, Largin and Robins, were arrested for the murder of Sarah's son, but although the proof was overwhelming—they were the only two who had fired into the crowd—no jury could be found to convict them, and they ended up being set free after an extended imprisonment.

Sarah Wunnuhhew, better known to us today as Sarah Doublet, was the widow of John Tahattawan, who was the son of "Old Tahattawan," the Massachusett Federation sagamore of the Nashobah. John was the sachem of Nashobah Plantation until his death around 1670. Sarah then remarried John Owannamug (Onamog), the ruler of the Praying Indians at Okommakamesit (Marlborough), but he died shortly thereafter. Sarah was of royal sagamore blood herself. She was the daughter of Sagamore-John, a sachem of the Wamesit.

Note 12: Sagamore-John of Wamesit is not to be confused with John Sagamore (Wonohaquaham), eldest son of Nanepashemet, or Sagamore John (Horowaninit), the Nipmuck Sachem of Pakachoog. Similarly, John Owannamug is not to be confused with John Oonsumog/Awassamug, the husband of Yawata, a daughter of Nanepashemet.

After Owannamug's death, Sarah remained in Okommakamesit, and if not presiding as their Squaw Sachem, she was certainly leader of a contingent from Wamesit who made their home with her.

In August of 1675, an incident happened that involved some Hassanamesit Praying Indians who were staying at the Okommakamesit Indian fort. In retaliation for the raid on Lancaster, Captain Mosley arrested 14 of them, including Old Jethro, and plundered the fort. This was effectively the end of Okommakamesit, and Sarah returned with her people to her childhood village of Wamesit. (Paul Brodeur, *Peaceful Indians Forced to Scatter*, Main Street Journal, Marlborough, December 12, 2016)

She is described by Gookin as having been "a woman of good report for religion" and was severely wounded in the attack. She would eventually marry Tom Dublet (Nepanet).

Note 13: The Wamesit Praying Indians had the misfortune of being near Chelmsford, which was particularly hostile to them as evidenced by petitions to, and orders from, the Great and General Court relative to them in a seven-week period of autumn 1675:

October 22, 1675: "Warrant to secure witness against the Wamesit Indians for certain outrages committed Chelmsford." (They were supposed to have burned a barn but hadn't.) (Massachusetts Archives, Volume 30, Page 183)

December 9, 1675: "Order for Captain Gookin & others to persuade the Indians at Concord & Chelmsford to settle at Deer Island." (Massachusetts Archives, Volume 30, Page 190)

December 13, 1675: "Petition of Wm Underwood & other of Chelmsford stating that they considered the return of the Wamesit Indian to be dangerous to their settlement and asking that they be disposed of elsewhere." (Massachusetts Archives, Volume 30, Pages 186-187)

Sometime during or after February 1676, the Wamesit left for Canada, leaving behind six or seven aged and infirm men and women. Once more, tragedy struck: Two men from Chelmsford burned these aged people to death in their wigwams, reportedly enjoying the notoriety of their act. (Drake and Bodge)

From Nashobah to Concord

By October of 1675, the popular intolerance against the Praying Indians was such that "the authorities and the friends of these Indians believed that it would be best to get them down to Deer Island" for their own safety, as related by Bodge.

The Nashobah Plantation Indians had been slated for Deer Island along with the Natick and others, but an attempt was made on their behalf that resulted in an order that they be send to Concord under the care and watch of John Hoar. Apparently, it was argued that there was not enough food and fuel on Deer Island to sustain them. As part of this agreement, the Nashobah were to "be kept employed for their maintenance and preserved from harm and the country made secure from them," as related by Hudson.

In Concord, a Committee of Militia was established in October, with Peter Bulkeley as chairman, until he was appointed in November to "attend the forces that are now to go forth against the enemy, and to be ministers to them." Bulkeley was not ordained, but he was educated in the ministry at Harvard and had preached for a year at Braintree. (Alfred Sereno Hudson, *History of Concord*, 1904)

John Hoar was also a member of the Committee of the Militia. He was the only lawyer in Concord, 53 years old at the time, and was a man of strong and unconventional ideas. He was a friend of the Indians, well-known and respected by them, and it is likely that he was behind the effort to have the Praying Indians of Nashobah brought to Concord instead of Deer Island, considering that it was he who provided the accommodations for them at his own expense. It is also likely that this offer to accommodate and pay for their upkeep had been part of the plan presented to the Governor's Council for approval.

Note 14: According to Walcott, "Hoar was an eccentric lawyer, well known, and correspondingly disliked, by the authorities, as a man of independent thought and a facile tongue, which was continually making trouble for him." (Charles H. Walcott, Concord in the Colonial Period, 1884)

Walcott footnoted several examples of Hoar's legal entanglements: "For uttering complaints that justice was denied him in the courts, he was compelled, in 1665, to give a bond for his good behavior, and was 'disabled to plead any cases but his oune in this jurisdiction.' (Mass. Records, iv. pt. ii. 292.) In 1668, he was fined £10 for saying 'at Ensigne Willm Busse his house that the Blessing which his Master Bulkely [Rev. Edward Bulkeley] pronounced in dismissing the publique Assembly in the Meetinghouse was no better than vane babling.' Subsequently, on two occasions at least, he was summoned into court to answer 'for neglecting the public worship of God on the Lord's days.'"(County Court Files, 1668, 1675)

The Hoars are connected to Littleton by way of the Reuben Hoar Library. The library was established by a bequest of William S. Houghton in honor of Reuben Hoar, who had assisted his father financially in a difficult period.

On November 19, 1675, the General Court agreed to the plan and ordered the Nashobah to Concord. Major Gookin and John Eliot, along with Major Simon Willard, as a committee of the court, were sent to carry out the removal and see them properly cared for (*Massachusetts Archives*, Volume 30, Page 185a).

This order came several days after the attack on the unarmed Wamesit women and children about 10 miles northeast of Nashobah Plantation. News traveled fast among the Indians, and they all knew John Tahattawan's widow and child—she had lived there among them until five years previously.

In autumn of 1675, the sachem of Nashobah Plantation was Captain Josiah (Pennahannit), who was "marshal-general or high-sheriff to all the Praying Indian towns, and attended the chief courts held at Natick and elsewhere, but dwelt at Nashobah," according to Shattuck in 1835.

Captain Josiah had been chief ruler of Nashobah after the death of John Tahattawan around 1670. It is unclear how he held the sachemship, for (if I understand the rules of succession), on the death of John, his widow Sarah, who was the daughter of John-Sagamore and therefore of royal blood, should have become Squaw Sachem of Nashobah. When she remarried her new husband, Owannamug, would become the sachem of Nashobah. With his death, it would revert back to her. It is unclear how John Tahattawan's son, had he lived, would have fit into the sachemship, or the role played by William Nahaton, said by some to be John's brother. (See note 24)

But the general rules of Indian succession, as laid out by Shattuck in his description of the sachemship of Musketaquid (Concord), were undermined in the Praying villages by Reverend Eliot's move toward an English-style governorship by appointment. It was part of his belief that for the Indians to become Christianized, they must first become Anglicized, as related by Thomas Hutchinson in his 1795 *History of Massachusetts*.

Note 15: The prevailing succession of sachemships is clearly outlined in Shattuck's 1836 The History of the Town of Concord, in his description of the rulers of Musketaquid of about 1621:

"Nanapashement was the great king or sachem of these Indians. ... He left a widow, Squaw Sachem and five children. Squaw Sachem succeeded to all the power and influence of her husband, as the great queen of the tribe. Her power was so much dreaded, when she was first visited by the Plymouth people in 1621, that her enemies, the sachems of Boston and Neponset, desired protection against her, as one condition of submission to the English. She married Wibbacowitts (Webcowit/Webcowites), 'the powwaw, priest, witch, sorcerer or chirurgeon' of the tribe. This officer was highest in esteem next to the sachem; and he claimed as a right the hand of a widowed sachem in marriage; and by this connexion became a king in the right of his wife, clothed with such authority as was possessed by her squawship."

After the devastation of King Philip's War and the fracturing of the Praying Indian villages, the traditional rules of succession reestablished themselves. We hear no more about Captain Josiah, but "Sarah Indian" (Sarah Doublet, wife of Tom Dublet) begins to loom large, and there is every reason to believe that she was none other than John-Sagamore's daughter Wunnuhhew and the widow of John Tahattawan, asserting her Squaw Sachemship over Nashobah.

Note 16: Sarah Indian [Sarah Doublet] is named—and is the only Indian named—when the town of Nashoba was incorporated in 1714, and as part of the documents of Incorporation, set aside a 500-acre reservation for the Indians: "And that Five hundred Acres of Land be reserved and laid out for the Benefit of any of the Descendants of the Indian Proprietors of the Said Plantation, that may be surviving; A Proportion thereof to be for Sarah Doublet alias Sarah Indian."

It seems unlikely that Sarah Indian would be given a legal "proportion thereof" unless she had some claim by inheritance or successionship. (The town name of Nashoba was changed the next year in 1715 to Littleton.)

However this was, in the fall of 1675, the Nashobahs' neighbors and relatives in Wamesit had been attacked by vigilantes, and their old friends Gookin and Eliot were asking them to move to Concord on behalf of the General Court. They may not have relished the idea of leaving their woodland home by the lake in Littleton for a barn in Concord, but the fear generated by the Wamesit shootings probably loomed large in their thinking. The Nashobah, under Captain Josiah, may well have viewed their move to Concord as a move to safety. They certainly did not retreat into the wilderness as the Wamesit had.

But the impending move to Concord caused, according to

Charles H. Walcott in his 1884 *Concord in the Colonial Period*, "a great commotion among the people [of Concord], for the memory of Brookfield [Quaboag Plantation] was still fresh, and the sight of an Indian was scarcely endurable." For those ill-at-ease with Indians in general—which it would seem was most everyone—having them in Concord itself simply exacerbated the situation.

The Nashobah Praying Indians, all but one of whom were to remain true to the English, were nonetheless escorted from Speen's End "between the waters" to Concord. They were, however, able to bring with them six months' worth of corn and their personal belongings. There were only 58 all told, "of not more than a dozen able bodied men and their families," according to Walcott. Nashobah Plantation now stood empty.

Gookin said that "In pursuance of this settlement, Mr. Hoar had begun to build a large and convenient work-house for the Indians near his own dwelling, which stood about the midst of the town." This was built at his own considerable expense.

John Hoar moved from Scituate to Concord in 1659 and set up practice as Concord's first attorney. After arriving, he purchased more than 300 acres across the Assabet River near the present Concord rotary. But in 1671 he sold most of this to Edward Wright in exchange for the usual "valuable consideration," including a good deal of Wrights land in town on Bay Road.

Here Hoar constructed a four-room manor house, two rooms upstairs, two down, which was large for the era. Behind John's manor house was the smaller tenant farmhouse of Thomas Fox.

Bay Road and the ridge behind it was the original site of Concord. In the first year of colonization, the English were reduced to constructing dwellings dug into the side of a ridge and covered with sod. The ridge is known as the Long Ridge, upon which they built their first meetinghouse, and extends easterly from Concord center along Bay Road (now Lexington Road).

Note 17: The Hoar manor is given a date of circa 1660, which does not fit with him having acquired the Bay Road property in 1671. The land he bought on arrival, the 300 acres across the Assabet, was well out of town and not a good location for a new attorney setting up business. I wonder if he built a separate dwelling on Bay Road after he moved to Concord in 1659. The circa 1660 date of the Hoar manor fits with this, as does his unusual land swap with Wright.

Not only do these structures still stand, but they are also quite famous in their own right. In 1857 Bronson Alcott purchased the Hoar manor and tenant farmhouse along with 12 acres of land, and combining the two buildings and adding on a bit, created Orchard House, where his daughter Louisa May Alcott wrote *Little Women* in 1868.

The Nashobah Praying Indians would have known the Hoar manor well. It is the only known structure still standing where we can place the Nashobah Praying Indians—not only that, but it has been preserved in a fashion redolent of its original construction. When Alcott bought the property, both buildings were in a state of disrepair, but although he made them habitable again he did not modernize them, writing in his journal: "I wish to leave untouched as far as I can the homely effect of the buildings and retain for them the air of antiquity, the picturesqueness which is theirs and in keeping with the past."

The Alcotts sold Orchard House to family friend William Harris in 1884, and in turn it was acquired by the Louisa May Alcott Memorial Association in 1912 and preserved. No major structural changes have been made since the Alcotts' time.

However, as Louisa's books began generating revenue, the interior was improved with such items as carpets and wallpaper, but the structure itself—particularly in the early years of Bronson's ownership—was much the same as when the Nashobah Praying Indians where there.

A visit there today will give you a very good sense of how the Nashobah Praying Indians knew it. And know it they did. We can assume that though their dwelling was the work-house, that they took part in the household chores at what is now Orchard House, and assisted with work on the grounds and buildings.

Gookin said that the work-house Hoar constructed for the Nashobah was not only near his own dwelling in the midst of the town, but also "very nigh the town watch-house." Presumably, the watch-house was on the high ground of the Long Ridge in vicinity to the Hoar manor.

"This house was made," said Gookin, "not only to secure those Indians under lock and key by night, but to employ them and to set them to work by day, whereby they earned their own bread." Here the Indians lived "very soberly, and quietly, and industriously, and were all unarmed; neither could any of them be charged with any unfaithfulness to the English interests."

But the townspeople were unhappy with this and within three weeks, the General Court on December 9, 1676, ordered Gookin, Willard, Eliot, and Danforth to persuade the Indians at Concord and Chelmsford to resettle on Deer Island of their own accord, as recorded in the *Massachusetts Archives*, Volume 30, Page 190.

Note 18: Such were the fear of reprisal among the Wamesit and the looming specter of Deer Island, that shortly after the November 15 attack by men from Chelmsford on the Wamesit women and children, they and their minister and ruler Numphow (who was married to Passaconaway's eldest daughter) fled and "wandered up and down the woods fearing to be murdered if they should continue there," as told by Drake. *They returned cold and hungry in December, at which time William Underwood and other Chelmsford men petitioned the General Court on December 13 that they "considered the return of the Wamesit Indian to be dangerous to their settlement and asking that they be disposed of elsewhere."* (Massachusetts Archives, Volume 30, Pages 186-187)

In February they felt compelled to pack their wigwams and gather up their goods and flee for Canada, sending a note back: "I, Numphow, and John Lyne, we send the messenger to you again (Wecoposit) with this answer, we cannot come home again, we go towards the French, we go where Wanalancit is; the reason is, we went away from our home, we had help from the Council, but that did not do us good, but we had wrong by the English. 2nd. The reason is we went away from the English, for when there was any harm done in Chelmsford, they laid it to us and said we did it, but we know ourselves we never did harm to the English, but we go away peaceably and quietly. 3rd. As for the Island, we say there is no safety for us, because many English be not good, and maybe they come to us and kill us, as in the other case. We are not sorry for what we leave behind, but we are sorry the English have driven us from our praying to God and from our teacher. We did begin to understand a little of praying to God. We thank humbly the Council. We remember our love to Mr. Henchman and James Richardson."

Those who fled Wamesit never found a haven in their wanderings. Numphow died, as did others of famine and sickness, and when they returned and surrendered after the war in August of 1676, some were accused of bearing arms against the English and were either sold into slavery or hanged.

A large part of the issue was that unlike the nearby frontier towns of Lancaster, Chelmsford, Groton, and Dunstable, Concord had never been garrisoned, and would remain ungarrisoned the length of the war. As such, it had limited ability to defend itself, and the town feared betrayal of its vulnerable state by the Nashobah to Philip's men. Most of the able-bodied men had volunteered or been impressed into service, leaving the old men, women, and children to defend the town. Constable John Hayward expressed the vulnerable position and the fear they were in in this letter to Governor Leverett on June 13, 1676:

"[The Indians] "may produce a great deale of damage to us that are resident in Concord; because we are afraid they are acquainted with the Condition of our towne, & what quantyty of men we have gon out; and which way they have gone ... I hope your honor will be pleased to take it into Consideration & send us some more strength to support us from our enemies; for we are in dayly fear; that they will make an assault on our towne." (*Massachusetts Archives*, Vol. 113, Page 193)

But the Nashobah proved themselves true; Concord was never attacked, much less on the Praying Indians' account. But it is likely that Philip knew of the vulnerability. Folklore relates that Concord never suffered directly from the war due to the high opinion the Indians held of Peter Bulkeley. He was considered a "man of spirit," and his town was left alone.

Note 19: *Also of note is that Lieutenant (later Captain) Thomas Henchman was the military commander of Chelmsford and was as highly regarded as Bulkeley. Both Henchman and Bulkeley would go on to purchase half of the Nashobah Plantation in 1686.*

The situation between the English and the Nashobah stayed like this for about two months, and went as well as could be expected. The Nashobah did nothing to alarm the English, and the English, although they chafed at the situation, learned to live with it. The Indians spent their days in gainful pursuits, and their nights locked up in the work-house. (Hoar referred to it as a fort.) For the moment, things were stable.

From Concord to Deer Island

This delicate balance was changed in February by the hand of Netus, the Nipmuck Captain. On February 1, he and his small band attacked and massacred the Eames family in Framingham. Twelve days later he struck again, this time in Concord Village (just seven miles from Concord Center), killing Isaac and Jacob Shepard and abducting their cousin Mary Powers. Sandwiched between Netus' raids, the town of Lancaster had been attacked and burned to the ground by a war party led by Monoco and Sagamore Sam.

The colonists' deepest fears were realized and a movement formed to rid Concord of the Praying Indians. Walcott said that "shortly after the murder of Shepard, some of the inhabitants secretly invited Captain Mosley to come with his company and remove the Indians from the town." Mosley, who was always ready for a fight and, according to Gookin, "quartered his company not far off at that time," showed up in Concord on February 20, a Sunday.

Mosley was a former privateer in the Caribbean, and had, in response to Dutch pirates operating north of Boston, been commissioned command of the expedition against them on February 15, 1674, by the General Court. On April 2, 1675, he sailed back into Boston Harbor with the pirates in tow after winning a sea battle. When King Philip's War broke out two months later, he was regarded as a popular leader but he had no military commission. Instead, he organized an independent company of volunteers, and within three hours enlisted 110 men, some of them his old privateers and shipmates, even including some of the pirates he had captured who had been released.

Once in town, Mosley demanded that Hoar turn over the Indians, and set a guard on their work-house overnight. When Hoar still refused to give them over the next day (Mosley had neither military commission nor court authority and was acting illegally), Mosley had the door broken down and led the Indians away. Some of his soldiers "Plundered these poor creatures of their shirts, shoes, dishes, and such other things as they could lay their hands upon," according to Gookin.

They were marched down Bay Road to Charlestown on February 21 under a guard of 20 men and then transferred to Deer Island. (This is essentially the route the British took on their retreat from Concord back to Boston on April 19, 1775.)

Note 20: *Captain Mosley was stationed near Concord and showed up about the time Mary Powers of Concord Village (who had been abducted when Isaac and Jacob Shepard were killed) would have ridden into town if she escaped back via Lancaster. Alternately, had Mary escaped via the Old Bay Path to Boston, she would be arriving about the time Mosley was arriving there with the Nashobahs. Either way, Mosley would have been on the spot to hear her "intelligence" of the Indians' whereabouts.*

The Nashobah Praying Indians arrived on Deer Island, far from their home in the gentle hills and valleys of Littleton, in the dead of winter, singularly ill-equipped to survive, with no food and most of their clothes and belongings stolen or left behind in Concord. What little they had, other than the clams they dug, was provided for them by the New England Company (more formally known as the Honorable Corporation for the Propagation of the Gospel in New England, residing in London), and boated out to them by Eliot or his helpers. According to Bodge, "The Corporation in London came to the aid of the friends of the Christian Indians, and their support greatly encouraged the better sentiment of the Colony; for they not only sent supplies and money for the Indians, but letters inquiring into the treatment of the Christian Indians." However, this help for the most part came too late.

Note 21: The Nashobah Indians were the only Praying Indians that were not court ordered to Deer Island. They were escorted there illegally by Mosley, though no effort was made that I am aware of to reverse this.

Their sense of dismay at being placed on the island—and without just cause at that—must have been overwhelming. And it wasn't just their dismay—both the Natick and Punkapoag Praying Indians also must have felt deeply betrayed. They, like the Nashobah, had done all as was required of them by Massachusetts Bay, and yet for their loyalty were sent into a harsh and undeserved exile. This betrayal no doubt ran deep, and no doubt runs deep today.

Part 2: Deer Island

Deer Island: Furnace of Affliction

It was a bad time to arrive. Not only was it winter, but some people in Boston wanted the Praying Indians removed farther still, as far away as Barbados to live as slaves.

On February 22, the Massachusetts Council was petitioned by Bostonians who were nervous about the growing number of Indians on Deer Island, requesting that they be removed "to some place farther more from us." In response, the Council, "Having seriously considered the state of the Indians now Confyned to dear island," ordered that guards be posted on the island to prevent both Indians from escaping and slavers from capturing them, and also that all the Indians be put to work, "some spinning, others to breaking up land to plant on, others to get fish and clams."

Being pressed into slavery was a real threat and was the unspoken subtext of the petition, just as the Nipmuck had warned the Praying Indians of Hassanamesit, according to Jill Lepore in *When Deer Island Was Turned Into Devil's Island*, Bostonia Magazine, 2006.

But the General Court made a bold move in favor of the Praying Indians, declaring by public proclamation that "these Christian Indians to be the allies and friends of the English by the olden treaty of 1643, made with their fathers, and never to this day broken by them or their children," as recounted by Bodge. However, this did not improve the conditions on the island itself.

Deer Island was a desolate isle in Boston Harbor, "covered in forest trees and used for the grazing of sheep," and its sandy soil unfit for agriculture, according to Justin Winsor in the 1880 *Memorial History of Boston*. It was windswept in the best of weather, and winter was hardly the best of weather. Gookin wrote of the Indians' "sufferings, (which were not few)" in a late December 1675 visit with Eliot to the Island: "The Island was bleak and cold, their wigwams poor and mean, their clothes few and thin." There was little to eat but "clams and shellfish, that they digged out of the sand, at low water." At the time of Gookin's visit, Deer Island was home to "five hundred souls," mainly Natick and Punkapoag.

. . .

Nashobah Indians on Deer Island

It was not long after this, in late February, that the Nashobah arrived on Deer Island, with little food or clothing, "there to pass into the furnace of affliction," as Gookin put it.

Of the Nashobah so interred, we know some by name: William Nahaton, possibly brother or cousin of deceased Nashoba Plantation Sachem John Tahattawan, Thomas Dublet (Nepanet), and Peter Conway (Tatatiquinea). The venerable James Speen, the Indian minister, whose name has become associated with the site of the actual Nashobah Village (Speen's End), had also been deposited on its cold shores.

We hear little of Tom Dublet before his removal to Deer Island, but he and others of Nashobah were soon to play a pivotal role in attempting to negotiate a peace between Governor Leverett and the Indian sachems.

Deer Island to Long Island

By March conditions on Deer Island had deteriorated so badly that Old Ahaton, the venerable praying sachem and minister of Punkapoag, petitioned the General Court for "permission to leave Deer Island for Long Island," which was more suitable for agriculture, because "their provisions were running low" and also because they were being "shot at and threatened" on Deer Island. (*Massachusetts Archives*, Vol. 30, Page 200a)

Although it is recorded that no action was taken on his petition, we do see on March 14 that due to the Praying Indians being "in great distress for want of food for themselves, wives & children," the General Court approved Captain Daniel Henchman's request to impound a boat for the Deer Island Indians to use for fishing *(Massachusetts Archives,* Vol. 30, Page 197*)*. Also of note, the Praying Indians on Deer Island are tallied in this document to be "about 400 lives."

But the transfer across the harbor from Deer Island to Long Island had already begun. A decree had been made on March 8, 1676, to get 100 Indians off Deer Island and move them across the harbor to Long Island (and other islands), presumably to improve conditions. (*Massachusetts Archives,* Vol. 30, Page 195)

This was not appreciated by Henry Mayer, a Long Island land owner, and he submitted a complaint to the Council against it. This compliant was read on March 20 but was denied, and the transfer plan went ahead under Henchman. (*Massachusetts Archives,* Vol. 30, Page 198a)

Mayer seemed to have had a change of heart, or at least accepted the inevitable; on March 29 he petitioned the General Court, asking that the "Indians should come and plant a parcel of land…upon Long Island" that belonged to him. He explained his previous resistance as the "fear and dread of the Indians that remains upon my aged mother and my wife was unwilling that they should come." But "upon more mature consideration" he was "willing that the Indians shall have liberty to plant one hundred acres of [my] land." (*Massachusetts Archives,* Vol. 30, Page 199)

But it wasn't until early April that Deer Island was at last completely abandoned for Long Island. We can narrow the time frame of the final transfers to around April 7. Eliot recorded having gone out in a boat that day, "sent by the Council to order matters at Long Island, for the Indian's planting." The Indians were either already there by then, or about to be moved.

But this in itself did not relieve the suffering of the Praying

Indians. In fact, conditions on Long Island do not sound much better than Deer Island. According to Gookin in his *Doings and Sufferings of the Christian Indians*: "When their able men were for the generality drawn forth to the wars, the rest, being nearly four hundred old men, women, and children, were left upon Long Island, in a suffering state. It was intended they should plant corn upon the Islands, and in order thereunto they made some preparations, expending their labor upon clearing and breaking up ground...yet the poor Indians were discouraged, and in want of all things almost, except clams, which food (as some conceived) did occasion fluxes and other diseases among then; besides, they were very mean for clothing, and the Islands were bleak and cold with the sea winds in spring time, and the place afforded little fuel, and their wigwams were mean. In this condition of want and sickness they were, after their men were sent for to the wars..."

Note 22: Deer Island is now a gigantic wastewater treatment facility for Boston. Its construction was opposed by the Nipmuck Nation, who protested that the state authorities not only dug up Indian graves, but did not honor the bones that lay under the soil, according to Gary McCann, a policy consultant for the Muhheconneuk Intertribal Committee on Deer Island (MICDI), and as reported in the September 10, 2009 edition of the Littleton Independent.

"How much more disrespectful of a people can you get than that?" asked David White, a member of the Chaubungagungamaug Clan, also interviewed for the article.

According to Jill Lepore, "In the early 1990s, Native Americans in New England began staging protests at Deer Island, opposing the construction of a sewage treatment center there. And today many are protesting the inclusion of the island in the Boston Harbor Islands National Recreation Area. A heated battle is raging between those who wish to preserve Deer Island as a sacred site, isolated from the public, and those who wish to open the island to tourists and to share its history with them." (When Deer Island Turned Into Devil's Island, Bostonia magazine, 2006)

Why Deer Island?

Deer Island was a terrible place, but the intention behind it was not. For all its tragedy, the Puritan fathers had given considerable thought and debate to the plight of the Praying Indians. It was clear that the Praying Indians were in danger from both the English and the uprising Indians. They had been attacked by both sides, and the longer the war went on, the more danger they were in of being killed by vigilantes of both sides. The governor and his council had to find a way to protect them from both the English and Indians—after all, by living in formal granted plantations, they were under Crown protection.

Their solution was to settle them on an island in Boston Harbor, out of the reach of reprisals from both the English and the Indians. To the cooler heads that governed Bay Colony, the Praying Indians were not seen as dangerous, but in danger. The issue with Deer Island was not that it happened or that it happened for a bad reason—but that it happened badly.

Note 23: Deer Island was Massachusett Indian territory at the time of King Philip's War, and continued to be so for at least 10 years after the interments. Around 1630, Winnepurkitt (Sagamore George), the sachem of Saugus and son of Nanepashemet, is recorded as being the proprietor of Deer Island. On March 19, 1685, Winnepurkitt's grandson of Nonupanohow (David) "relinquished his rights to Deer Island." It would appear that Deer Island was held by Nanepashemet's family until at least 1685. (Charles Edward Beals Jr., Passaconaway in the White Moun-

tains, 1916; Ron Wiser, Ron Wiser Research Home Page, July 2000)

Where the situation became a tragedy and a fiasco was the lack of logistical support. The Praying Indians were without shelter, adequate clothing, food, and fuel. What little was brought to them by Eliot and others was just that—little. There were about 500 Indians, and starvation and exposure took their toll. No one had factored in or carried out the regular provisioning and supplying of the island. Eliot and his helpers would row out with supplies, but how much can a rowboat bring to aid 500 cold and hungry souls?

And when true support did come, it came far too late. Gookin, in his *Doings and Sufferings of the Christian Indians in New England*, said that in December of 1676, six months after they had left the island, "The widows and the aged had supply of clothing and corn at the charge of the Honorable Corporation in London, who tenderly and compassionately ordered relief for such as were in need."

Yet for all this, the Praying Indians did not outwardly turn on Christianity or the English. Gookin says of his several visits to Deer Island in December of 1675, "I observed in all my visits to them, that they carried themselves patiently, humbly, and piously, without murmuring or complaining against the English for their sufferings, (which were not few)." Instead, they fatalistically provided their services to the English to help spy on and fight Metacom and his allies. The words of Joseph Tukapewillin echo faintly here: "it is better to die than to fight the church of England."

According to Harwood, "William Nahaton, or Tahattawan, a brother of John Tahattawan, was among the Indians at Deer Island, and was one of the six selected to serve as guides under

Major Savage, in March, 1676." The Savage expedition was the one launched by Governor Leverett after Mosley received information from Mary Powers, the abducted girl from Concord Village, about the whereabouts of the Indians she had escaped from. At least one of her Nashobah Praying Indian neighbors, William Nahaton, was part of the effort to punish those who had killed her kinfolk, Isaac and Jacob Shepard.

Note 24: There is some question as to whether William Nahaton is the son of Old Ahaton, sachem of Punkapoag (Canton), or of Old Tahattawan of Nashobah.

First, there are a number of variations of both names due to the English spelling the Indian names as they sounded. Shattuck gave these variations for Tahattawan: Tahattawants, Attawan, Attawance and Ahatawance, to which Harwood added Tahattawarre and Nattahattawants. To this Drake added Tahatooner, and Hudson recorded the variants Atawans, Tohuttawun, and Tahuttawun.

For Ahaton, the variations are Ahauton and Nahaton, to which Mandell added Hahawton. (Daniel R. Mandell in Behind the Frontier, 1996)

In calling William the brother of John Tahattawan, Harwood, it would seem, is drawing on Gookin's 1677 An Historical Account of the Doings and Sufferings of the Christian Indians in New England, in the Years 1676-1677. Gookin has two references to William, spelling his name Nahaton in one, and Ahaton in the other. The 1835 edition footnotes the Ahaton spelling with, "A name variously written, and very often beginning with an N. He was son of Tahattawan, Sachem of Musketaquid, since Concord." The footnotes are credited to Samuel G. Drake, and he is assumed to have started the theory that Ahaton and Tahattawan are the same.

Hudson, in his 1904 History of Concord Massachusetts, follows Harwood's lead and says, "William Tahattawan, brother of John the Chieftain, although among those who were exiled to Deer Island, served as a faithful guide of Major Savage, a Colonial officer."

However, in his Brief Narrative in 1670, Eliot says that Tahattawan of Nashobah had only one son, who "was elected to rule in his father's place, but soon died." Further, in discussing the praying village of Punkapoag, Eliot refers to the ruler as Ahauton and his son as "William, the son of Ahauton." Also, Sachem Ahauton would seem to be the "Old Ahaton" who petitioned the General Court while on Deer Island.

Both Tahattawan and Ahauton are described by Eliot as being sachems of the blood (Sagamores) and of similar character. Tahattawan is a "strict yet gentle ruler" and Ahaton is "more loved than feared." But they can't be the same person; Ahauton was on Deer Island in 1676, and Tahattawan had died before 1670.

Ahaton and Tahattawan are probably variations of the same name, and Old Ahaton and Old Tahattawan were presumably related, if not brothers. If so, there were strong ties between Punkapoag and Nashobah, similar to the familial ties that existed between the leaders of Nashobah and Natick.

Note 25: The Massachusetts Archives relate a case of adultery concerning William Ahaton's wife on November 11, 1668, excerpted as such: "Examination by Daniel Gookin of Sarah Ahaton (Indian wife of William Ahaton) accused of committing adultery with another Indian named Joseph. Sarah was impris-

oned briefly but pleaded with the court to free her since her husband was willing to take her back." Once released, Sarah was so depressed and humiliated that she climbed a large rock in Punkapoag and jumped headfirst to her death.

Running Out of Food

Scarcity of food was not just an issue on Deer Island. In the early spring of 1676, the situation on the mainland had become desperate for both the Indians and the English. As spring planting approached, both the Indians and the English needed to divert manpower to the fields if there was to be any grain that autumn. This was more critical for the Indians, who, though they had the manpower advantage over the English, had neither the provisions nor the resources for a protracted conflict, and who were running a highly mobile guerilla-type war that greatly interfered with food production. There was also the issue that their fields and food caches were routinely destroyed by the English.

The English still had plenty of relatively safe farmlands in and around the Bay, but they did not have enough men to work the farms and fight the Indians at the same time. Famine was a real prospect for both the English and the Indians.

Governor Leverett needed more fields put under cultivation to provide for the hundreds of refugee families that had fled their burned-out towns, but this would pull men from the military, a move he couldn't afford. As it was, able-bodied men resisted recruitment because they needed to start the spring planting and others deserted to their farms for the same reason, leaving towns and garrisons under-protected at the most critical time, according to Dennis Cannole in his 2001 book *The Indians of the Nipmuck Country in Southern New England 1630-1750*. Cannole goes on to say that selectmen were given power by the General Court to "impress men for the management and carrying on of the husbandry of such persons as are called off from the same into the [military] service." Each town was given the power to put the less able-bodied men to work on the farms and the more able-bodied in the military. But it came with a catch—the military men had to pay the farm workers 18 pence a day.

The Indians had food problems of their own, and the sachems ordered the women, children, and elderly to divide into small bands and replant their fields, and others to go to rivers and lakes and catch fish.

Peace Talks

It was against this backdrop of an impending grain shortage that the governor and other high-ranking Bay Colony officials sought to end the war through negotiation. They had been considering this since January 1676 when they had learned from the Praying Indian James Quanapohit that "some of the Nipmucks, especially the 'Chief Men and old men,' were inclined toward a peace and wanted to discontinue the fighting," according to Cannole.

In early April, Governor Leverett and his council came to the decision to initiate talks with the Indian sachems, not only to work towards a truce, but also to negotiate the release of English prisoners. The council approached Daniel Gookin and asked him to enlist the help of the Praying Indians on Deer Island to courier letters back and forth from Boston to the Wachusett camp of the Nipmuck sachems and Metacom.

Once again Gookin went to Deer Island to recruit, but according to Bodge, "At first it was impossible to find any one of the friendly Indians willing to venture as messenger among the hostiles, mainly because they had been so cruelly and shamefully abused by the English." Earlier it had been easy to recruit, but not anymore, primarily because the six Praying Indians that had volunteered as scouts in late February, "were so insulted and abused" by their troop-mates during their time as scouts "that they returned to the Island [so] utterly discouraged," that no one was willing to work for the English again "for a long time."

Tom Dublet: Negotiator

In the end it was Tom Dublet who consented to go. Gookin knew him from Nashobah Plantation, and on April 3 Dublet set off for Wachusett with a letter from the governor, and some ink and paper for the sachems' reply. The letter offered to redeem captives "either for payment in goods or wampum or by exchange of prisoners." Leverett also opened the door for peace negotiations and instructed that any emissaries they sent would not be harmed if they came unarmed and waving a "white flag upon a staffe, visible to be seene," as instructed in his March 31, 1676, letter to the sachems by Governor Leverett.

Note 26: The old records show a variety of spellings of Tom's name: Dublet, Dublett, Dubelet, and Doublet, and his Native name is variously spelled Nepanet or Neepannum. Mostly he is referred to as Tom Dublet, and I have standardized my text with this spelling, and the Nepanet spelling of his Native name.

Dublet proved good at the task, eliciting a written response for the sachems at Wachusett: Sagamore Sam, Old Jethro, and the Sagamores Kutquen and Quanohit. The letter was transcribed by Peter-Jethro, a literate Praying Indian who had sided with the Nipmuck. His father, Old Jethro, was a Praying Indian minister from Okommakamesit (Marlborough) and had switched sides as well, after having been roughed up by Captain Mosley.

Earlier in 1675, when Mosley and his pirates had heard about the August 22 raid on Lancaster in which seven people were slain, he in turn raided the unarmed Praying Indians of Okommakamesit (whom he unfoundedly believed had been responsible) and took 14 or 15 captive, including Old Jethro and two of his sons, Peter-Jethro being one of them. He tied them together by their necks and marched them to Boston. This was not the last time Old Jethro would be walked down the streets of Boston with a rope around his neck, but the next time would be his last.

Note 27: Some sources have 11 or 15 Indians detained by Moseley, but the number at trial was 14. Mosley had a reputation as an Indian killer, but it would appear he spent a good part of his time illegally rounding up innocent, unarmed Praying Indians at his own behest. He was Governor Leverett's brother-in-law and was never sanctioned or reprimanded for his activities, which had popular support.

The captives were held in Cambridge in prison and stood trial at the Court of Assistants (an assistant was akin to a senator) on September 21, 1675. Of the 14, all stood trial for murder at Lancaster, with the exception of Old Jethro, who was up on charges of abusive speech from an earlier incident in Groton. Of the 13 tried for Lancaster, one was found guilty and hanged, and three were "sent away" to the Barbados. Both of Old Jethro's sons were acquitted.

We don't know the full circumstances of Old Jethro's trial, but the records of the Court of Assistants indicate that he was tried for "abusive" and "wicked speeches uttered by him in Mr. Willurds yard at Groaton." For this he was convicted and sentenced "to be whipt with thirty stripes." All of the acquitted were ordered to Natick to be released by Waban. Old Jethro was sent with them to be whipped.

This indicates that all were indeed Praying Indians, as they were being remanded to Waban in Natick.

Note 28: Peter-Jethro's name was probably Paguskmeut. I surmise this from the trial records where there is only one Peter named, "Peter, alias Paguskmeut."

It is difficult to get a consistent narrative from the various accounts that mention the incident. The generally accepted narrative is that although Old Jethro's and his sons were acquitted of the Lancaster murders, they were yet ordered to Deer Island, escaping from prison in Cambridge the night before they were to be transported to the island, and were so angered by the entire ordeal that they then joined the Nipmuck against the English.

But the court records clearly show that the trials took place in late September, and the first interments on Deer Island did not occur until October 30. What seems to have happened is that Old Jethro, his sons, and the other acquitted were indeed remanded to Natick where Old Jethro presumably received his punishment. When the Natick Praying Indians were not long after ordered to Deer Island, it appears that Old Jethro swiftly departed Natick with his entire family (according to Gookin) and took up with the Nipmuck. His son Peter-Jethro switched sides with him, although he would redeem himself in the end like a Judas, turning in his own father to the hangman.

In terms of Tom Dublet, after an exchange of letters between the Wachusett Nipmuck sachems and the Bay Colony officials, Tom was joined in his efforts by Peter Conway (Tatatiquinea), another Nashobah Plantation Praying Indian who was released from Deer Island, to assist in the negotiation efforts. Releasing English captives was high among English priorities for negotiating peace; they were not going to the negotiation table until all the captive English had been freed. The first on the list was Mary Rowlandson, who had been captured at Lancaster three months earlier and had been kept as a slave by Weetamoe, the sister of Wootonekanuske who was Metacom's wife.

Note 29: Weetamoe was Squaw Sachem of the Pocasset, the warrior tribe of the Wampanoag. Her husband at the time of King Philip's War was Quinnapin, a Narragansett sachem. She had previously been married to Wamsutta (Alexander), who was Chief Sachem of the Wampanoag Confederacy, and brother of Metacom. After Wamsutta died, Metacom became Chief Sachem.

The Wachusett sachems were willing to release Mary Rowlandson for a price, and on April 28, the council asked Tom and Peter to escort John Hoar of Concord, who was well-known and respected among the Indians, out to Wachusett to finalize the deal and bring Mary back. Hoar seems to have inserted himself into the proceedings, and Mary Rowlandson described his arrival: "On a sabbath day … came Mr. John Hoar, (the council permitting him, and his own forward spirit inclining him,) together with the two fore mentioned Indians, Tom and Peter."

Hoar arrived amid a hail of bullets. Some of the young braves amused themselves by firing at his horse's hooves and over its head, nearly bucking Hoar off, and then shoved him around for a while. Mary Rowlandson described the scene: "They shot over his horse, and under, and before his horse, and they pushed him this way and that way, at their pleasure."

Once the roughhousing was over and the hungry sachems had gotten a taste of the food that John brought for them, Quinnapin, Mary's master, agreed that he would let her go it is said for a pint of liquor.

Although the records of the time do not directly state it, the release of Mary appears to be due in a large part to the diplomacy of Tom Dublet. He appears to have been a skilled envoy, and through his efforts Bay Colony was able to achieve the release of the rest of the English in captivity.

The communication between both sides was by letters. The English would send a letter with Dublet, and the Indians would send one transcribed by Peter-Jethro back with him. But he was no simple mail-carrier; the success of the endeavor rested as much on the contents of the letter as on the comportment of the carrier. He had to carry the process through to the sachems reading the letters favorably, and then to getting favorable replies from the Sachems to the letters, in turn. Hidden between the lines of these replies to Leveret's letters was Dublet's diplomatic skill.

Throughout the freeing of the English prisoners, Governor Leverett had never lost sight of the main objective, which was to negotiate a truce. Tom was directly involved with this, moving the groundwork forward one step at a time.

"If you will send us home all the English prisoners it will be a true testimony of a pure heart in you for peace," wrote Governor Leveret to the sachems, as recorded in the *Massachusetts Colony Records*, Vol. 5, Page 83.

The first objective was finally accomplished and almost all the captives returned to their homes. (*New England Deliverances*, the Rev. Thomas Cobbet of Ipswich, *New England Register*, Vol. VII, Pages 209-219)

"Resolved to make war theire worke"

By early May, the Nipmuck sachems were no longer in complete accord with their Pokanoket ally, Metacom, and were indicating that they were ready to talk peace, according to Cannole. In a letter, Governor Leverett acknowledged the Indians' wish for a cease-fire to plant corn and again invited the

Wachusett sachems to an in-person talk. "You desire not to be hindered by our men in your planting, promising not to do damage to our towns. This is a great matter and cannot be ended by letters without speaking one with another." (*Massachusetts Colony Records*, Vol. 5, Page 83, also Pages 93-94)

Note 30: *The once-powerful alliance between Metacom, the Pokanoket Chief Sachem of the Wampanoag Confederacy, and the Nipmuck Sachems, had been aided by the fact that Metacom's mother was a Nipmuck of the Quaboag band.*

Toward this end, Leverett had already established that he did not want to sit down at the table with the Indians "in the open woods" and that he requested the meeting be in Boston, or if not, "in some convenient garrison" in Concord or Sudbury. (*Massachusetts Colony Records*, Vol. 5, Page 83, also Pages 93-94)

By now, Leverett had involved two Englishmen, Jonathan Prescott and Peter Gardiner, in the efforts to set up a negotiation table. These two worked with Tom Dublet to extend yet another offer of safe conduct to the sachems to come to Concord to civilly resolve matters.

Unfortunately, this is the last we hear of the English effort to negotiate a truce; we can only conclude from the lack of other official documents that their offer was rejected, and military means proceeded to a final conclusion. (The Indians tried brokering peace several times later, but by then the war was a foregone conclusion in favor of the English and these last-minute advances were disregarded.) The English had been up-front with the sachems in letters, saying that if the Indians rebuffed their efforts for peace, they were "resolved to make war theire worke until they enjoy a firme peace." It would appear the Indians took them up on making war their work.

Or did they? Both Sagamore Sam and John Monoco, like most of the Nipmuck war leaders, were leaning toward a truce. It was Metacom who continued to fight. According to Ellis and Morris in *King Philip's War* (1906), Monoco and Sam "declared later that they were inclined toward peace." The release of the English prisoners by the Nipmuck angered Metacom, who felt they were needed as bargaining chips. This disagreement drove a wedge between the Nipmuck and Metacom's Pokanoket, which significantly hastened the end of the war.

Drake said of it: "It is certain that this negotiation was the immediate cause of their final overthrow." This is because "this parleying with the English was so detestable to Metacom that a separation took place" where he split from the Nipmuck and "he and the Narragansets [see notes 30 & 31] went off to their own country." Drake added that this "is the reason they were so easily subdued after the separation took place."

Note 31: Drake was incorrect about Metacom being Narraganset; he was Pokanoket Wampanoag.

Although the Nipmuck were inclined to peace, Metacom and his Pokanokets fought on alone, but as far as the English were concerned, the war wasn't over until Metacom was killed or called a truce. But without the Nipmuck support, Metacom had no chance in battle.

However, before the rift between the Nipmuck and the Pokanoket became irreparable, a face-to-face peace negotiation actually happened. There are no official records of the meeting. It is only known because about eight years after the event, Jonathan Prescott and Daniel Champney wrote a letter to the General Court on Tom Dublet's behalf, asking him to be rewarded for the service he gave Bay Colony at this important meeting.

Prescott, Gardiner, and Champney

The meeting was a face-to-face negotiation between Bay Colony representatives Peter Gardiner, Jonathan Prescott, and Daniel Champney, and most likely the Wachusett sachems who had been exchanging letters with Governor Leverett about peace talks and prisoner releases over the past month: Sagamore Sam, Old Jethro, and Sagamore John. Tom Dublet acted as interpreter.

Jonathan Prescott was 33 years old and originally from Lancaster. He was in the Prescott garrison with his parents and children during the February 10 attack by Monoco, but afterward moved to Concord and married Elizabeth, the daughter of John Hoar. He was described as a man of energy and influence and was highly respected, being much involved in the public sphere. He became a captain in the militia sometime after the war and represented the town of Concord in the General Assembly for nine years. His star seemed to have ascended after he married attorney John Hoar's daughter in 1675.

What little we know of Peter Gardiner (Gardener) begins with what James Savage wrote in his *Genealogical Dictionary of the First Settlers of the New World*, published in 1862: "Peter Gardiner of Roxbury embarked in April, 1635, on the Elizabeth, at London. He died November 5, 1698. His son Samuel was killed by the Indians April 2, 1676."

Gardiner was born in 1617 in England and was 59 at the time of the peace mission. He lived in Roxbury at the junction of Warren and Dudley Streets. His son Samuel was part of Captain Isaac Johnson's company that included the 52 Praying Indians enlisted at the beginning of the war, among whom were brothers James and Thomas Quanapohit. Samuel was killed on April 21, 1676, at the Sudbury fight, not on the April 2, 1676, date that

Savage has. (The negotiations were held about six weeks after his son was killed.)

About Daniel Champney is even less information. The most I can surmise from the sources available (Bodge's *Soldiers in King Philip's War*) is that he lived somewhere near the Charles River in Boston, and after the Praying Indians were released from Deer Island in May of 1676, some of them were settled near his farm "and employed to cut wood and build stone walls, while the women were taught and then employed as spinners," according to Bodge. There was also a Daniel Champney who was part of the Middlesex Company, but I don't know if this was one and the same person.

All three were connected with the Praying Indians in some way. Gardiner's son had served in a company with them, and Champney was a sympathizer and protector, as was Prescott via his father-in-law, John Hoar. The negotiation mission Champney undertook with Prescott and Gardiner happened after the Praying Indians who were released from Deer Island had come to live on his farm.

None of these three Englishmen were high-level officials; in fact they don't seem to have been government officials at all. There is no indication as to why they were chosen for this important meeting. Yet in a letter to the General Court on April 2, 1684, by Prescott and Champney, in reference to this meeting, it appears they were indeed working at the behest of the Governor's Council: "Wheras wee Peeter Gardner, Daniel Chamney, & Jonathan Prescot were Imployed By the Hono'ed Council sometime in May or June 1777...." (*Massachusetts Archives*, Vol. 30, Page 279)

Negotiations in Nashobah

The letter to the General Court explains that Tom Dublet had bargained for the release of Goodman Moss [John Morse of Groton], having gone to Wachusett "to treat with the enemy, and procured them to meet us about twenty miles from there quarters for the Sachem met us between Concord and Groton."

What the letter is saying is that Tom had gone to Wachusett to negotiate a meeting with the sachems and had secured their word to meet Prescott and Champney about 20 miles from Wachusett, and that they did indeed meet with the Sachems at a place between Concord and Groton.

Note 32: The original document is in the Massachusetts Archives, Vol. 30, Page 279. This is a handwritten document from 1684, and is quite aged and difficult to read. In the transcribed and printed versions, there is a significant missing detail: The transcribed versions read "for the sachem met us between Concord and Groton." But in the original document, there is a letter in superscript after the word sachem, much in the way that "ye" is written in these old documents as "y^e." The letter appears to be a plural "s," which makes it sachems, or in the format of the original, **Sachem^S***. It is hard to decipher, but where a word is inserted between two other words, the writer used a caret. In this instance, there is no caret, but a letter that appears to be an "s" in superscript.*

It is significant because the level of importance of the meeting is dependent on how many sachems attended. If it was a one-sachem meeting, the meeting was of lower significance than if there were more in attendance. I read it as a plural "s", but I cannot be completely sure this is accurate. Other transcribers have simply ignored it.

Governor Leverett had established that any formal meeting would not be in the "open woods" and if not held in Boston, then "in some convenient garrison" in Concord or Sudbury. The actual meeting took place at a location between Groton and Concord. It certainly was not held in Groton; Groton had been burned to the ground and abandoned in March, and there were no longer any functional garrison houses there.

There was, however, one garrison standing not only between Groton and Concord, but also about 20 miles due east of Mount Wachusett. This was the Powers garrison house in Concord Village, from which Mary Powers had been abducted in February. In fact, it was the only garrison standing west of Concord. So most likely the meeting took place in the Powers garrison at the foot of Nashoba Hill with Tom Dublet serving as "interp'ter & helper in that Affayre" that took place on his home ground of Nashobah Plantation.

Note 33: Wachusett is a Natick word that means "near the mountain." The Wachusett camp was probably in the area east of the mountain and south of the lake—but it was not on the mountain itself, as some have erroneously theorized. (John C. Huden, Indian Place Names of New England, 1962)

The letters from Leverett instruct the sachems that in a truce negotiation, they were to carry "A white flag upon a staff, visible to be seene" to signal their intentions and acquire safe conduct. It is likely that when the Wachusett delegation arrived, they came down the old Indian path that is now Great Road carrying aloft such a white flag.

The meeting occurred sometime around June 2 because Captain Henchman, who was stationed at the military post of Concord, recorded on that day that, "Tom Doublet went away soon after Mr. Clark, and with him John Prescott, Daniel Champney & Josiah White, carrying the pay [ransom] for

Goodman Moss." This also indicated that Concord had served as the logistical base of the negotiations.

Note 34: Josiah White is a new name in the affair but is not mentioned in the letter from Prescott and Champney to the General Court as being part of the negotiating team. He seems rather to have been involved in the ransom of Moss. All I can gather of him is conjecture. He may have been the son of John White who lived near Muddy River in Boston, who, like Champney, had taken in Praying Indians after their release from Deer Island in May. He may have served in King Philip's War, and may be the Josiah White who became prominent in Lancaster after it was resettled.

Other than this letter to the General Court eight years after the fact, there are no known records of the meeting. Nevertheless, this was the first and only face-to-face peace meeting that happened between the English and the Indians in King Philip's War. The entire episode seems to have been buried and forgotten under the exchange for Moss. Even Harwood, his 1895 article in the *Proceedings of the Littleton Historical Society,* saw no more in it than a ransom exchange and inferred it was transacted at Tom Dublet's hut on Beaver Brook. On the other hand, Dennis Cannole picked out the negotiation meeting hidden under the ransom exchange in *The Indians of the Nipmuck Country in Southern New England 1630-1750.*

The meeting does not seem to have been a successful one. No further attempts at a truce were made by the English, and the war came to a military conclusion two and a half months later with Metacom's demise.

It is an easy task to identify the location of the meeting place as the Powers garrison in Concord Village. It fits the descriptions in the Prescott and Champney letter and the state of affairs at the time. We also know who was there on the English side: Prescott, Champney, and Gardiner, and their interpreter Tom Dublet. But we don't know which sachems participated. We can assume they were some of those whom the negotiators had been dealing with all along: Sagamore Sam, Old Jethro, and Sagamore John. But was Metacom, King Philip himself, involved at this meeting?

Starting with the release of Mary Rowlandson on May 2, 1676, which Metacom attended, he became increasingly more incensed with the Nipmuck sachems' parleying with the English and releasing prisoners. This eventually led to a split between the Nipmuck and Metacom and his Pokanoket warriors, and they decamped from Wachusett. It seems unlikely that he would be involved, so dead-set was he against negotiating with the English. As well, he was a proud man. If he were to negotiate, he would only do so with his English counterpart, Governor Leverett.

For Tom Dublet's efforts, and thanks to the letter from Prescott and Champney, Tom was awarded two coats from the legislature.

Note 35: Following is the full transcript of the Prescott and Champney letter and the response of the council (Massachusetts Archives, Vol. 30, Page 279):

April the second 1684: Whereas wee Peeter Gardner, Daniel Chamney & Jonathan Prescot were Imployed By the Hono'ed Council somtime in May or June 1677 [1676] To goe vp among The enimy Indians that then quartered in the woods About Watchuset in order to procure the deliuery of Inglish Captiues. Wee doe Certify that Thomas Dublet alius Nepanet was our interp'ter & helper in that Affayre; And that hee had beene a jorney before that time to treat with the enimy & had procured them to meet vs, aboue twenty miles from ther quarters for the sachem^s met vs betwene Concord & Groaten; And at that time old Goodman

Moss of Waterton [Groton] was deliuerd to vs & brought home & haueing By order paid fower pounds for his redempti[on] which Thomas Nepan[et] had bargaind for in his forme[r] jorney, And wee further say ye the said Tom Nepanet carried it faithfully in that matter & Deserues satisfaction for his Trauile & Adventure in ye dificult time & wee vnderstand hee hath receiued no satisfaction for that seruice hitherto, therefore wee humble conceue the Honored Councill should consider, him & order him to receue thirty or forty shillings for that Hazardoes seruice: And In testimony of the Truth of this certificate wee whose names are aboue exposed haue hervnto sett our hands, the day & yeare aboue written.

To bee p'sented To the Honble Gouemor & Councill of the Massachusetts Colony; by the pson Concerned.

Jonathan Prescott
Danil Chamne

At a Council held at Boston the 8th May 1684 In Answer to the petition of Tho Dublett Indian & in sattisfaction for his paynes & trauile about ye procurmet of Goodman Morses freedom from ye Indians Its ordered that ye Tresurer Giue him two Coates

E R S [Edward Rawson, Secretary of the Colony]

Part 3: After Deer Island

Release from Deer Island

Eventually the harsh winter began to turn to spring, and the cold of the Praying Indians on Deer Island, and after that Long

Island, abated, but the hunger continued. The six long months of freezing temperatures and starvation had taken their toll, and tragically, not all the Praying Indians stranded on the islands survived to see the spring. But even the arrival of spring did not end their misery. By this time, they were so weakened that they could no longer care for themselves and "being ready to perish for want of bread" were "incapacitated to make provision for the future," according to Jill Lepore in *Bostonia* magazine.

But by May, the tide of war was swinging irrevocably in the English's favor and with the new victories and less fear, a more Christian attitude toward the Praying Indians was developing. Gookin reported that by mid-May, "God was pleased to mollify the hearts and minds of men towards them, by little and little," and that the "the hearts of many were in a degree changed to those Christian Indians; and the General Court then sitting passed an order, giving liberty to remove them from the Islands."

Toward the early spring, the Praying Indians were removed from Deer Island to Long Island. Deer Island was unfit for agriculture; Long Island was more suitable for planting corn "and in order thereunto they made some preparations, expending their labor upon clearing and breaking up ground," as related by Gookin.

A Praying Indian company of 42 men had been drawn up under Captain Hunting and was deployed on April 21 in time to serve in the Sudbury fight, and that number increased to 80 men shortly afterward. Bodge referenced the transfer from Deer Island to Long Island when referring to the men of Captain Hunter's company: "But when this number of able-bodied men were drawn forth from the Christian Indians, there were left upon Long Island, whither they were now removed, some four hundred old men, women and children."

The first we hear of the Nashobahs since they were sent to Deer Island comes from the *Massachusetts Archives*, Vol. 30, Page 201b. On May 10, 1676, an order from the General Court was issued that "for the better protection of the Indians that the Punkapoag be moved to Milton and the Natick and Nashobah Indians near the falls in the Charles River." This is only a court summary of the order, but it is nonetheless the order that released the Praying Indians from the islands.

It is significant to see that of the 14 villages that were sent to the islands, only three, the Nashobah among them, were still cohesive enough to be named. This indicates the degree to which they survived their exile intact as a group; it may indicate that the Praying Indians on Deer Island were for the most part from the Old Villages of Natick, Punkapoag, and Nashobah.

The order to release the Praying Indians from the islands was given on May 10, and by May 12 they were off the island as related by Eliot: "Day 12th the Indians came off the island—Capt. Gookin cares for the them at Cambridge." (First Church Records, Roxbury)

Once released from the island in late May, the surviving Indians were divided into two groups, those of the Old Villages and those of the New Villages. The Nashobah were among the Old Villagers, who spent the summer in Cambridge "near the falls of the Charles River." This was on the lands of Thomas Oliver, "which was very commodious for situation, being near Charles river, convenient for fishing, and where was plenty of fuel; and Mr. Oliver had a good fortification at his house, near the place where the wigwams stood, where (if need were) they might retreat for their security," as Gookin put it in his *Doings and Sufferings*.

Some of the Old Villagers were then dispersed into smaller

family groups in nearby towns, such as the family that stayed with Daniel Champney near the Charles River. For the most part, they were "employed to cut wood and build stone walls, while the women were taught and then employed as spinners," according to Bodge.

But even getting off the islands did not ease their suffering. As Gookin related, "This deliverance from the Island was a jubilee to those poor creatures; and though many of them were sick at this time of their removal, especially some of the chief men, as Waban, John Thomas, and Josiah Harding, with divers other men, women, and children, were sick of a dysentery and fever, at their first coming up from the Island; but by the care of the Major [Gookin, referencing himself], and his wife, and Mr. Elliot, making provision for them, of food and medicines, several of them recovered, particularly Waban and John Thomas; the one the principal ruler, and the other a principal teacher of them, who were both extreme low."

Note 36: *Note that Gookin says, "though <u>many</u> of them were sick", he then added that "<u>several</u> of them recovered." The difference between "many" and "several" implies that not only did some Indians not recover, but that it was more than a few who died. This is a significant admission. It is the only source document of the era that I know of that admits—even if in a roundabout way— that Indians died during, or due to, their interment on Deer Island.*

The Nashobah at Concord

By October the Old Villagers were moved again, this time back to or near their old plantations, although for the most part, those who survived Deer Island came to live at Natick or Punkapoag. Some stayed on with the English they had lived with during the summer and made lives among them. But the

Nashobah Praying Indians chose to return to Concord and "lived outside English households," and worked for the English, many as servants in their homes, according to Daniel R. Mandell in *Behind the Frontier*, 1996. They were kept, Gookin said, "under the inspection of the committee of militia and selectmen."

But even so, paranoia could still run high. On June 13, 1676, Governor Leverett received a letter from John Hayward, a constable in Concord, who warned that three squaws had escaped from the town and he was worried that the squaws would "inform their tribe of the layout of the town." (*Massachusetts Archives*, Vol. 30, Page 203a)

Murder at Hurtleberry Hill

Far more troubling was the murder of six Praying Indian women and children on August 7 of 1676, which occurred on the northern end of a hill said to be about a mile south of Walden Pond. This was a small family group consisting of Andrew Pittimee's wife, her sister who was the wife of Thomas Speen, and four of the Speen's children, including a baby. They had only come from Deer Island 3 months before, and were living at the falls of the Charles River in Cambridge. In want of food, they had been given permission by Daniel Gookin to venture out and pick hurtleberries.

The women and children encountered a group of English from Concord on patrol, four of whom circled back later and murdered them; some hacked to death in the head with hatchets. The four Englishmen—Stephen Goble, Daniel Goble, Nathaniel Wilde, and Daniel Hoare—all from Concord, were quickly imprisoned. They were tried and confessed to the deed, and sentenced to be hanged. But only the Goble men were actually hanged. Both Wilde and Hoare were later pardoned on appeal in murky circumstances. Thomas Speen was the brother of James

Speen, the Praying Indian minister of Nashobah Plantation. (*Records of the Court of Assistants of the Colony of the Massachusetts Bay, 1630-1692*; Daniel Gookin, *An Historical Account of the Doings and Sufferings of the Christian Indians*, 1677)

The motivations of the murders must have been complex, and are disturbing, as evidenced by the brutality of the attack and the fact that one of the guilty was Daniel Hoare, the son of John Hoare [Hoar] of Concord who had sheltered the Nashobah from Deer Island for three months at his own expense. Daniel lived with his father at that time, and would have known the Praying Indians on close personal terms. It is deeply disturbing that he was involved.

Surviving Deer Island

The Nashobah Praying Indians began their trek through the furnace of affliction on November 19 of 1675, when all told, 58 men, women, and children were first removed to Concord. A year later, on November 10, 1676, six months after they had been released from the islands and returned to Concord, Gookin reported "their number may be about fifty."

Assuming the missing eight people represent deaths, and these deaths were related to their interment on Deer Island, this is an 86.2 percent survival rate for the Nashobah. However, this is only an estimate; there are many variables, especially since Gookin seemed unsure exactly how many Nashobah were in Concord in 1676.

But by this reckoning, (imprecise though it is), it would seem they did not suffer as much on the island as the other Praying Indians. This is most likely because they weren't interred there until February 21, 1676; they were only on Deer Island for three months and missed most of the winter. Most of the other Indians had been there for a good six months, throughout the entire winter—such as the Natick, who were there from October 30, 1675 to May 12, 1676, a total of about 28 weeks, or six and a half months. Although all suffered hunger, sickness, and exposure, the Nashobah were spared half of it—so it reasons that their survival rate would be higher than that of the Natick and Punkapoag.

Nashobah Plantation Fades

Nashobah Plantation never recovered from King Philip's War and never became a thriving village again. Gookin reported in November of 1676 that the Nashobah Indians, about 50 in number (10 men, 40 women and children), had resettled in Concord and were living there quietly and unmolested. But this peace seems to have been short-lived.

Part of why they never returned to Nashobah Plantation as a group was because of the Mohawk raids that followed hard on the King Philip's War. The war had triggered long-standing hostilities between tribes of the Massachusett Federation and the Mohawks, and the Mohawks began a war against the already-devastated New England Indians. The safest places the Praying Indians could find were the English population centers, and there they settled and lived. When the English and the Mohawk came to an agreement, the Praying Indians quietly faded back to Natick or Punkapoag by September of 1677. Consolidated there, they had enough numbers to effectively resettle and man forts. But not all left; some few stayed with the English as servants.

An interesting anecdote about the Nashobah Indians at this time concerns a drought in the summer of 1676. Carolyn Webster in her May 1957 *Littleton Legends* column related that the drought was so bad that "Prayers of rain were said even by the Indians and finally the rains came."

By 1684, Nashobah Plantation is described in the *Massachusetts Archives*, Vol. 113, Page 193, as "inhabited by a small parcel of Indians, but for many years hath been deserted, all dead except some few yet are dispersed." Two years previous to this, what were left of the Nashobah had begun selling off the plantation to the English.

In January of 1705, James Speen petitioned the General Court to get compensation for a musket taken from him in August of 1675. In this petition he identifies himself as "James Speen, Indian of Nashoba." This document reveals Speen was living in Nashobah in 1705.

But on November 15, 1702, Bulkeley, Henchman (Thomas, not Daniel), Powers, and Whitcomb, who had between them bought the entirety of the old Indian plantation, were confirming their 1686 purchase of land from the Nashobah and in the Massachusetts Archives described Nashobah Plantation as "A certain tract of land called Nashoby … that was reserved and confirmed as a township for the Indian Proprietors thereof, who afterwards removed themselves and families to Natick and having no occasion for their lands at Nashoby, they and their descendants that remain, and are now reduced to very few…" (*Massachusetts Archives*, Vol. 30, Page 486)

There are several points of interest in this. Bulkeley, Henchman, Powers, and Whitcomb, the progenitors of the future Littleton Proprietors, stated that the plantation was empty of Indians and that they had all moved to Natick. However, James Speen earlier in the year was giving his address as Nashobah. The Indian plantation itself was entirely sold and gone, and yet Speen was still living there. In 1685, he was recorded as "old Speen" (*Massachusetts Archives*, Vol. 30, Page 305).

This would become a significant issue 12 years later when the town was incorporated; the Indians had sold, but some were still living there on the land anyway.

Along with Speen, one of the few who stayed, or at least would come and go, was Tom Dublet and his wife Sarah Indian (Wunnuhhew). He lived in a hut near his fishing hole on Beaver Brook, across the street from Joel Proctor's house: "Near the family residence was the wigwam of Thomas Dublet, one of the Nashobah Indians, well known and friendly to the early settlers; and upon lands adjoining or belonging thereto many interesting Indian relics have been found." (Obituary of Joel Proctor)

Fragments of one such relic, one of Tom Dublet's pots, can be seen at the Littleton Historical Society.

Note 37: According to Harwood, who relied on oral traditions related by Joel Proctor, the hut "was located near Mr. Proctor's house, and just across the street...his [fishing] 'hole' a short distance down the brook." This would place the hut on the west side of Beaver Brook near where it is bridged by Great Road. The hut would have been just upstream of the bridge and most likely on the banks. The pot fragments were kept by the Proctor family who were early settlers in town, and gifted by Joel Proctor to the Reuben Hoar Library. (Harwood, Herbert J., Littleton Historical Society, Proceedings No. 1, 1894-1895, 1896)

Sold as Slaves to Jamaica and Barbados

It is a fact that many of Indians who fought against the English were sold as slaves to the West Indies, as were some of the Praying Indians. In post-King Philip's War New England, there were typically only three fates for the captured Pokanoket, Nipmuck, and their allies: They were pardoned, executed, or sold as slaves. The enslavement and deportation of rebellious individuals had been declared legal and was seen as a simple method of dealing with a complex situation. In the English view, it got the "troublemakers" out of the Colony for good and avoided mass executions.

Enslaving Indians did not become a regular practice until after the war, when large numbers of warring Indians were captured or surrendered, but it had been going on to an extent up to that point. Indeed, it was an English practice during the Cromwellian wars to send the Irish to Jamaica and Barbados as slaves.

By the end of King Philip's War, the practice intensified and became a regular procedure with at least 1,000 Indians, most out of Plymouth, sold in its direct aftermath to Jamaica and Barbados. In an odd twist, not all the slave ships out of Plymouth were welcome in the West Indies. One such ship that set out following King Philip's War ended up discharging its human cargo in Africa. (Nathaniel Phillbrick, *Mayflower: A Story of Courage, Community and War*, 2006)

The Rev. Eliot was against the selling of the Indians—any Indians. He preached and lobbied against it early, as the *Massachusetts Archives* show the receipt of an August 13, 1675, letter read in the legislature "from the Rev. Mr. Eliot protesting against selling Indians as slaves."

For Eliot's efforts on behalf of the Praying Indians and Indians in general, he and Gookin became targets, receiving death threats and attacks, Gookin in particular because he had grown up in Ireland. Eliot related that Gookin was afraid to walk the streets, and on Election Day "the people in their distemper left out Captain Gookin and put him off the Bench." (First Church Records, Roxbury)

Note 38: Even though Gookin was English, his having grown

up in Ireland was used again him by his ill-wishers. On February 28, 1676, in a case that went to court, private Richard Scott called him an "Irish dog that was never faithful to his country, the sonne of a whore, a bitch, a rouge, God confound him, and God rott his soul," and added, "If I should ever meet him alone I would pistol him. I wish my knife and sizers were in his heart. He is the devil's interpreter."

On one occasion, on April 7 of 1676, when Eliot was ferrying supplies to the Indians in Boston Harbor, he was intentionally rammed by a larger vessel and nearly drowned.

Note 39: Eliot related the experience: "Captain Gookins, Mr. Danforth, Mr. Stoughton were sent by the Council to order matters at Long Island, for the Indians planting – in our way thither, a great boat of about 14 tun, meeting us, turned hard upon us (whether willfully or by negligence, God, he knoweth.) I so sunk I drank in salt water twice and could not help it." Mr. Danforth was deputy governor of Massachusetts, and Mr. Stoughton was chief justice of the province. (First Church Records, Roxbury)

Note 40: In the First Church Records, Eliot gave the date of the incident as "1676, on the 7th day of the 2nd month." This is an Old Style dating convention given in the Julian calendar system. In Old Style, the first month is March, making the second month April, and the day, the 7th of April. The year remains 1676, because after March the Julian and Georgian calendars were back in relative synchronization, year-wise. This is corroborated by the Genealogy of the Descendants of John Eliot, 1905, which give the date as April 7, 1676.

Detainment and deportation in slavery were legal in Bay Colony but only under government authority. It was initially a punishment for crime, not an industry, although some in authority began to see it as a means of replenishing the coffers that had been decimated by the war.

Although there was legally no private enterprise allowed in this way, this did not stop slavers from skirting through and grabbing what Indians they could. This became such a concern for the Praying Indians on Deer Island, where they were vulnerable to slave ships, that in early March the council ordered that guards be posted on the island to prevent slavers from capturing them. (This also served the dual purpose of preventing escapes.)

Death of the Praying Sachems

Many of the Indians were deported as slaves, but execution was reserved for "all such as have been notoriously cruel to women and children, so soon as discovered they are to be executed in the sight of their fellow Indians," as outlined in emissary Edward Randolph's report of the war to King James II.

By August of 1676, while the Nashobah were recuperating by the falls of the Charles River, King Philip's War had wound to a close and King Philip—Metacom—had been killed. The sachems of Wachusett had been captured as well, and colonial justice brought to bear. These included Sagamore Sam, Monoco, Captain Tom, Old Jethro, and Mattoonus.

Note 41: Sagamore Sam's wife was taken prisoner and brought in by Tom Dublet.

Captain Tom was the first praying sachem to go. He was brought in on June 10, 1676, and after a trial in Boston, was hanged on June 22, as noted by Eliot, who was with him at his death. He was remembered well by the Praying Indians of Captain Hunter's Company, if by no one else. They petitioned the

General Court on his behalf, and Gookin said of Captain Tom that he must have been "tempted beyond his strength."

Eliot said about this about the execution: "I accompanied him to his death; on the ladder he lifted up his hands and said, I never did lift up hand against the English, nor was I at Sudbury, only I was willing to go away with the enemies that surprised us. When the ladder was turned he lifted up his hands to heaven prayer-wise, and so held them till strength failed, and then by degrees sunk down."

Samuel Drake, often an unsympathetic writer, commented that "Capt. Tom's case was one of most melancholy interest, and his fate will ever be deeply regretted; inasmuch as the proof against him, so far as we can discover, would not at any other time have been deemed worthy of a moments serious consideration."

Mattoonus was next. He and one of his sons had been captured and brought to Boston on July 27 by Sagamore John, who on turning himself in used Mattoonus to bargain for his own pardon for his parts in the war. In the shifting alliances that characterized the difficult position the Praying Indians found themselves in, Sagamore John had been sagamore of the Praying Indian village of Pakachoog, and Mattoonus his constable.

The English had been long incensed at Mattoonus and condemned him to immediate death. Sagamore John, seeking to solidify his new-found favor with the English, asked to execute Mattoonus with his own hands. This was granted, and he took Mattoonus to Boston Common, bound him to a tree, and there "shot him to death," according to Drake, who is quoting Mather. However, Samuel Sewell recorded in his diary that "Sagamore John comes in, brings Mattoonus and his sonne prisoner. Mattoonus shot to death the same day by John's men."

Old Jethro (Tantamous) was the last, the one Nashobah Praying Indian who in the English view went renegade. He was captured with Monoco and Sagamore Sam. On September 26, William Hubbard observed Monoco "with a few more Bragadozio's like himself, Sagamore Sam, Old Jethro, marching towards the gallows with an halter about his neck, with which he was hanged at the town's end," and recorded the event in his *Narrative of the Indians Wars*. Hezekiah Butterworth adds in the 1893 *Popular History of Boston* that he was hanged from the old elm that stood at the end of town near the waters of the Charles.

As for Old Jethro, he was captured with Monoco and others who had gone at his son Peter-Jethro's request to Major Waldron at Cochecho to make peace, but was seized and sent to Boston. Speaking about Peter-Jethro, Increase Mather said, "That abominable Indian, Peter-Jethro, betrayed *his own father*, and others of his special acquaintance, unto death." It seems Peter-Jethro *had* been negotiating with the English for his own skin; the council instructed Gookin to "Tell James the Printer [Peter-Jethro] and others, to bring in the heads of the Indians as a proof of his fidelity." Indeed, he brought in his own father, and was subsequently pardoned. (*Massachusetts Archives*, Vol. 30, Page 207)

Old Jethro—Tantamous in his native tongue—was a complex figure in a complex time. Not only was he a Praying Indian minister, but was a powwow as well, residing on Nobscot Hill, about halfway between Nashobah and Natick. He did not seem to be playing at either side, but appears to have been sincere, with commitment to both the old ways and his ministerial duties.

His defection to Metacom was not a betrayal so much as an angry man declaring himself and his values openly at a crossroads of history. He was clearly angry and speaking his mind openly of the English. His trial for "wicked and abusive utterances" are proof of this. Add to this his harsh treatment by Moseley followed by his imprisonment, conviction and punishment—and the sudden threat of Deer Island—and it's not hard to see why he chose the way he did. But it was more than a choice, it was a statement.

Note 42: Gookin had considered Old Jethro several years earlier to be a "grave and pious man" and sent him out as a missionary, but after King Philip's War he backpedaled and said: "but this man and his relations were not Praying Indians, nor did they live at Natick, only since the wars, but dwelt at a place near Sudbury, Nobscot Hill, and never submitted to the Christian profession, but separated from them, being sons of ill fame, and especially the old man, who had the repute to be a powow; those ran away for fear at this time, and were with the enemy."

Note 43: Some accounts make James the Printer the son of Naoas and the nephew of Joseph Tukapewillin; others say he is the same person as Peter-Jethro.

Lost Guns

When the Natick Praying Indians were ordered to Deer Island, they were given but an hour's notice, and left many of their possessions behind. Bodge relates that "their neighbors, the English, as soon as they had left their homes, immediately fell upon their villages and robbed them of everything they left behind ... Their guns, hunting-gear, ammunition, stores etc., all which was their own property, were plundered by their English neighbors and never returned to them."

Indians, Praying or not, were not supposed to have firearms; it was made illegal in the Colony in 1633. But by 1657, Bay Colony began to license the selling of "guns, swords, powder and shot" to the Indians, "by which means the Indians have been abundantly furnished with great store of armes and ammunition to the utter ruin and undoing of many families in the neighbouring colonies to enrich some few of their relations and church members," as wrote Edward Randolph in his report to King James II on the war.

He then went on to cite the case of Captain Tom: "And at Natick there was a gathered church of Praying Indians, who were exercised as trained bands, under officers of their owne; these have been the most barbarous and cruel enemies to the English of any others. Capt. Tom, their leader, being lately taken and hanged at Boston, with one other of their chiefs." (There is no evidence that the Natick Praying Indians were as a whole or in bands, enemies to the English.)

Note 44: Randolph blamed the English for their misfortunes in part, saying: "for they first taught the Indians the use of armes, and admitted them to be present at all their musters and trainings, and shewed them how to handle, mend and fix their muskets, and have been furnished with all sorts of armes by permission of the government, so that the Indians are become excellent firemen."

The same plundering occurred in Concord by Mosley's men when they marched the Nashobah to Charlestown in February. Due to the atmosphere of distrust and outright hostility, the Nashobah most likely had had their firearms confiscated when they first arrived in Concord.

However, there is a tantalizing glimpse of a more noble role that that the Governor's Council saw for the Praying Indians. A week after they arrived in Concord, the Governor's Council had ordered the "selectmen and militia of Concord" to "employ the Nashoba Indians as a means of security for the town." There is no indication whether this was put into effect or not, but I doubt it, based on the prevailing emotions of the time and the fact that although the government and military officers saw the value of the Praying Indians, the bulk of the population were hostile to them. (*Massachusetts Archives*, Vol. 30 Page 185a)

But we know they had guns and that they lost them. In January of 1702, James Speen petitioned for compensation, the original document for which is preserved in the State Archives: "Petition of James Speen in behalf of himself & others Indians of Nashobe [Nashobah] asking for compensation for guns taken from them by Lt. Ruddck [Lieut. John Rudduck]." This was followed by "testimony of Thomas & John Brigham concerning the guns and ammunition taken from James Speen in the war time."

However, this didn't happen in Concord, but in Marlborough. James Speen and other Praying Indians had apparently been part of Captain Isaac Johnson's company of 52 Indians that was drawn up in early July 1675 at the behest of Gookin, and rode out to join Major Savage at Mount Hope. At least 28 of this company participated in fighting Metacom's warriors at the Siege of Quaboag Planation (Brookfield) in early August of 1675, although they got no historical credit for this.

Speen said, in his petition to the General Court, "I the said James Speen Indian of Nashoba ... with many other Indians were employed & engaged against the common Indian enemy, at Mount Hope, & afterwards at Quaboag, in which engagements some of our Company lost their lives."

Up to this point, it was known only that there were some Indian guides with Captain Wheeler, James Quanapohit for one; but Speen's petition implies that there were at least 28 of Johnson's Praying Indian Company in Quaboag. Speen, and perhaps other Nashobah Indians, were deployed in the same company as Samuel Smedley, whose sister Mary was married to Isaac Shepard. Smedley was killed in the first fusillade in the ambush, which was subsequently known as "Wheeler's Surprise."

Note 45: Captain Thomas Wheeler, looking for the enemy Indian camp of Sachem Muttawmp, chose to cross a swamp to it in single file. The Indian guides, James Quanapohit and James Speen among them, protested against it, believing it was a trap. It was — and in the initial volley, Samuel Smedley was killed. The English were thrown into confusion, their captains seriously wounded. The entire company would most likely have been wiped out if not for the Praying Indian guides, one of whom took command and lead the rest of the company out of the swamp and into the hills.

Note 46: Captain Isaac Johnson died in the Narragansett campaign and Captain John Jacob of Hingham became the new commander. But it is unclear to whom the Praying Indians at the Quaboag fight were attached.

After Quaboag, the Praying Indian company was in Marlborough, which was garrisoned by Lieutenant John Rudduck. An attack on August 22 in Lancaster had killed seven people, and another Indian under duress by Moseley implicated the Hassanamesit Praying Indians, who were gathered at the Praying Indian fort in Marlborough. According to Bodge, "the popular clamor was so loud against them that Lieut. Ruddock, in command of the garrison at Marlborough, demanded the arms and ammunition of the whole body of Indians to be given up … an act entirely without the sanction of the Court."

We have Speen's view of the same event in his petition: "Lieut. John Rudduck signified to us that we were ordered by the

Honored Council to deliver our arms and ammunition into his hands for a few days, he promising to return them."

Not all of the Indians wanted to give up their arms, but they were persuaded by Speen himself and gave up the "number of twenty eight" to Rudduck. These firearms were never returned, and when he asked Rudduck, Speen was informed that "the English sold them to who liked them." Speen then made application to the council, which ordered the guns be "returned to the Indian owners, yet two only have been returned." Following this, Gookin made a promise that "if the other guns could not be found, satisfaction thence be made to us for them, but yet we have received none." Speen, in his petition, then asked the council to look into the matter on the behalf of himself, the remaining Indians, and the children of the ones who were now dead. (*Massachusetts Archives* Vol. 30, Page 489)

The testimony of Thomas Brigham was to the effect that the guns were delivered up by James Speen and about 20 Indians, and "promised they should have them again within a short time." This is followed by John Brigham, who testified that he "could get back two of them" but "the others were lost in the time of the war." (*Massachusetts Archives* Vol. 30, Page 488)

There is no indication if Speen and the others ever got satisfaction in the affair.

The Rudduck account is significant to the story of Old Jethro and Captain Tom. After all the Marlborough Indians' guns had been confiscated, Mosley showed up and plundered the Praying Indian fort. He arrested 14 Indians and sent them, tied neck to neck, to Boston for trial. Old Jethro and his son Peter-Jethro were among those sent to Boston, and after being remanded to Natick —Peter-Jethro acquitted and Old Jethro whipped—they were suddenly faced with deportation to Deer Island. Under such circumstances, it's not shocking that they joined Metacom's camp, allied against the English.

After this, the Hassanamesit staying at the Indian fort also felt so abused by Mosley and the English that many, when the Nipmuck pressured them to come with them—and with the threat of Deer Island looming above them—went quite willingly, including Captain Tom. James Speen, however, made his escape and remained true to the English.

Reward for Tom Dublet

Tom Dublet received no reward for this service to the English in King Philip's War. He had not been eager to volunteer, but when he finally agreed to Gookin's request, he gave his service wholeheartedly. And although he wasn't formally rewarded, he did get off Deer Island in the process.

Eight years later, in April of 1684, Jonathon Prescott and Daniel Champney wrote the governor and council of Massachusetts Bay Colony on Tom's behalf, saying of him that he "Deserves satisfaction for his trials and adventure in the difficult time and we understand he hath received no satisfaction for that service hitherto."

Dublet wasn't asking for much, and Prescott and Champney requested the council to consider that he "receive thirty or forty shillings for that hazardous service."

At a council meeting held six days later, it was indeed ruled to compensate Tom for his service: "In answer to the petition of Thomas Dublet Indian and in satisfaction for his pains & trial ... it is ordered that the Treasurer give him two coats." The document is signed "E R S" which stands for Edward Rawson, Secretary [of the Colony]. (*Massachusetts Archives*, Vol. 30, Page 279)

Tom's name is spelled both Dublet and Doublet, making it somewhat ironic that he was given coats. A "doublet" was a hip-length, snug-fitting, buttoned coat that was worn through the mid-17th century. Did the council perhaps say, "Let's give Dublet some Doublets"?

His name suggests that such a coat was a favorite piece of apparel. Indian names were difficult for the English to pronounce, and they instead called them by an English first name, or by an appellation that reflected them in some way, like "James-the-Printer." Tom's English name is essentially Tom-who-wears-a-doublet.

There is some humor in the reward, and it is hard to say if it was intentional or not, but at least these coats were something he liked to wear. I, for one, hope he derived satisfaction from them.

CHAPTER 3
SARAH DOUBLET'S INDIAN NEW TOWN

AFTER KING PHILIP'S WAR, FROM 1676 ONWARD, THERE WERE repeated efforts to characterize Nashobah Plantation to the General Court of Massachusetts Bay as being deserted of Indians, and to thus open the way for it becoming an English township.

In 1684 Nashobah Plantation was described as being "inhabited by a small parcel of Indians, but for many years hath been deserted, all dead except some few yet are dispersed." (*Massachusetts Archives*, Vol. 113, Page 193)

When Henchman, Powers, and Whitcomb moved to legalize their Indian deeds in 1702 they stated that the Nashobah Indians had "removed themselves and families to Natick and having no occasion for their lands at Nashoby ... and are reduced to very few."

The 1702 Stow petition for annexing Nashobah declared that it "for a long time hath been and still is deserted and left by the Indians none being now resident there." (*Massachusetts Archives*, Vol. 113, Page 330)

The next petition to the court for Nashobah, made in 1711, described it as "practically deserted by the Indians" and is a "considerable tract of land lying vacant and unimproved." (*Massachusetts Archives*, Vol. 113, Page 603)

This is true to the extent that most of the Praying Indians of Nashobah Planation had moved to Natick following King Philip's War in 1677. But there was always a small presence that remained, or came and went from Natick with the planting and gathering seasons. For instance, Thomas Dublet was residing there in the 1680s and James Speen, the Indian minister, had made it his home by 1701.

Although Nashobah Plantation by then was not a functioning village, its sachemship was still a point of pride among the Indians of the lineage of old Tahattawan, who was a sagamore of the royal blood. In fact, it was the sachemship that the Indians believed had the power to make land sales to the English.

Following King Philip's War, the civil-style government that Eliot had instituted in the Indian plantations had reverted back to a rule by sachem as in the old days. This change was driven by both the Indians and the English, as explained by Daniel R. Mandell in the *Behind the Frontier*, 1996: "aboriginal leadership remerged after resettlement [following King Philip's War], in part from the Indians needs and desires, and in part because provincial officials (and their legal system) found Sagamores, Sachems, and their heirs useful in obtaining land."

This is exactly what we see in the 1686 Bulkeley-Henchman Indian deed where the lineage and right to the land is proclaimed in the opening lines of the deed: "Kehonowsquaw alias Sarah, the daughter and sole heiress of John Tahattawan, Sachem and late of Nashobah deceased; Naanishcow, alias John Thomas;

Naanasquaw alias Rebeckah, wife to the said Naanishcow; Naashkinomenet, alias Solomon, eldest son of said Naanishcow and Naanasquaw, sister to the aforesaid John Tahattawan; Weegrammominet alias Thomas Waban; Nackcominewock, relict of Crooked Robin; Wunnuhhew alias Sarah, wife to Neepanum alias Tom Dubelet."

This delineation of lineage was also the line of succession of the sachemship of Nashobah, and the ranking demonstrated the degree of relationship between the signatory in the deed and old Tahattawan, John Tahattawan's father, the sagamore of the blood. The closer the relationship (and thus the closer in line to the Sachemship the person was), the higher their name is found on the deed.

Conditions and Provisions

The Great and General Court had passed acts to prevent the Praying Indians from selling their land and becoming destitute. One such act, called *An Act to Prevent and Make Void Clandestine and Illegal Purchases of Lands from the Indians* (passed on June 26, 1701) was designed with "the intent Native Indians might not be injured or defeated of their just rights and possessions, or be imposed on and abused in selling and disposing of their lands, and thereby deprive themselves of such places as were suitable for their settlement and improvement."

When the Court legalized the Bulkeley-Henchman, Powers, and Whitcomb deeds on October 15, 1702, they did so provisionally; they did not take the petitioner's word that Nashobah Plantation was no longer inhabited by Indians. In fact, they had received an earlier petition from James Speen that very year on an unrelated matter in which he gave his name and residence as "I James Speen of Nashobah." The Court knew Nashobah was not deserted of Indians.

The provision for confirming the Indian deeds was that the petitioners "agree with the Indians yet remaining upon ye place for a convenient settlement." The abstract in the *Massachusetts Archives* is even blunter: "House resolved to grant the petition provided a place was maintained for those Indians who wished to stay."

When the Nashobah Plantation lands were once again petitioned to the General Court in 1711 to be made into an English township, the same issue arose again. The petitioners described the plantation as being "practically deserted" of Indians, but the Court was doubtful and convened a committee on May 30, 1711, to "view the land mentioned in the petition." There were a number of tasks given to the committee, the issue of the Indians not the least of them.

The committee acted with unusual speed and reported back to the Great and General Court a week later on the 7th of June. They reported that there were "two or three families only remaining" of the Indian proprietors of the plantation.

One can assume that whatever "convenient settlement" was made for the Indians by Court order in 1702 was most likely where these several Indian families were living when the committee came out to view the land.

The Great and General Court of the Province of Massachusetts Bay incorporated the Nashobah lands as an English township on November 2, 1714, and named it Nashoba. Like the confirmation of the deeds in 1702, this Act of Incorporation was provisional, as well. There were three requirements: that the town "be settled with thirty-five families," that an "orthodox minister" be settled among them within three years, and that acreage be set aside for the remaining Indians.

The provision for the Indians' acreage is in the Act of Incorporation itself: "that five hundred acres of land be reserved and laid out for the benefit of any of the descendants of the Indian proprietors of the said plantation, that may be surviving; a portion thereof to be for Sarah Dublet alias Sarah Indian."

Note 1: The Act of Incorporation also included the provision that "The Rev. Mr. John Leveret & Spencer Philips Esqr. to be Trustees for the said Indians to take care of the said Lands for their Use."

Who Was Sarah Doublet?

One of the most puzzling questions is, who was Sarah Doublet? We only hear of her a few times in the official records of the era, mainly in deeds, of which there are four. The first is a 1684 deed to Major Samuel Willard, next in the 1686 Bulkeley-Henchman deed, then in the 1714 Act of Incorporation, and last in 1736 in her deed to Elnathan and Ephraim Jones of Acton.

Clearly she looms large over the Indian New Town. Indeed, she is singled out by name to receive a portion of it. There is no one else named but her. So who was she, and why this distinction?

Sagamore-John

Sarah Doublet's name was originally Wunnuhhew. She was of royal lineage, the daughter of Sagamore-John who was the "staunch friend of the English," sachem of the Pawtucket village of Wamesit (Chelmsford/Lowell). Drake identified her in 1854, saying "She [Sarah] was daughter of Sagamore-John, who lived and died at the same place [Wamesit]." This was affirmed by Herbert Harwood in the 1896 *Proceedings of the Littleton Historical*

Society: "John Tahattawan died before 1670, and left a widow Sarah, daughter of Sagamore John of the Wamesits." (Samuel Gardner Drake, *History of the Early Discovery of America*, 1854)

Sarah was known as "a woman of good report of religion," and her father, also known as John-of-Wamesit, was remembered as having been a "great friend of the English," as recorded by Drake.

Following Sagamore-John's death sometime between 1658 and 1660, Numphow (Nobhow), a "prince of the blood" who had married Passaconaway's eldest daughter, became sachem of the Wamesit (Charles Edward Beals Jr., *Passaconaway in the White Mountains*, 1916). During King Philip's War, Numphow led the Wamesit northward into the wilderness, seeking safety with Passaconaway's son Wonalancet.

These relationships indicate that the Wamesit sachemship was linked to Passaconaway, and that Sagamore-John was either of Passaconaway's line or had married into it like Numphow.

Passaconaway had been under the Grand Sagamore of the Massachusett, Nanepashemet, and all this together means that Sarah was a Pawtucket band Indian of the Massachusett Federation, and of the royal line. Hudson made the Pawtucket connection explicit when discussing a 500-acre tract in Shabokin (Ayer) that Major Simon Willard obtained in 1658 "in satisfaction of a debt of £44 due from John, Sagamore of Pawtucket." (Hudson, Alfred Sereno, *The History of Concord, Massachusetts, Volume I, Colonial Concord*, 1904)

Note 2: Sagamore-John is not to be confused with John Sagamore (Wonohaquaham), the eldest son of Nanepashemet, or with Sagamore John (Horowaninit) of Pakachoog. John-Wonohaquaham was the sachem of Mishawum (Charlestown) and died of the plague in 1633. John-Horowaninit was a Nipmuck, also known as Abigganosh or Quaqunquaset. Also, Sagamore-John was not "John Lyne" as some have speculated. Lyne was alive in King Philip's war in 1675, and Sagamore-John had passed by 1660.

Rules of Succession

As a member of the royal line, Sarah-Wunnuhhew would only marry others of her rank in the Massachusett Federation. So it was not surprising that she married John Tahattawan (occasionally referred to as John Tahatooner), the son of Sagamore Tahattawan in nearby Musketaquid. Old Tahattawan's principal seat was *Nashope*—Nashobah—and his son John became its sachem in turn.

This put Sarah in the successorship queue of sachemship over Nashobah.

This is evident from the old deeds alone. According to Mandell, after King Philip's War the old sachemships reemerged in the Praying Indian community in part because the English system of land-title was best suited to dealing with the sachems and sagamores, or their heirs, in land transactions. These, of course, first had to be cleared by the General Court.

As such, it was more expedient to have title derived from the traditional Indian rulers of the land in question. The other reason was that the Indians themselves preferred their traditional leadership system of bloodline sachemship over the Eliot-introduced English civil style of governance.

. . .

That meant that in Nashobah for an Indian to have sale rights or inheritance rights over the land, he had to have been related to old Tahattawan along certain succession rules.

These rules of succession of sachemship are clearly outlined in Shattuck's 1836 *The History of the Town of Concord* in his description of the rulers of Musketaquid (Concord) of about 1621:

"Nanapashement was the great king or sachem of these Indians ... He left a widow, Squaw Sachem and five children. Squaw Sachem succeeded to all the power and influence of her husband, as the great queen of the tribe. Her power was so much dreaded, when she was first visited by the Plymouth people in 1621, that her enemies, the sachems of Boston and Neponset, desired protection against her, as one condition of submission to the English. She married Wibbacowitts, 'the powwaw, priest, witch, sorcerer or chirurgeon' of the tribe. This officer was highest in esteem next to the sachem; and he claimed as a right the hand of a widowed sachem in marriage; and by this connexion became a king in the right of his wife, clothed with such authority as was possessed by her squawship."

This successionship was in play in Nashobah, especially in the 1686 Bulkeley-Henchman deed: "Kehonowsquaw alias Sarah, the daughter and sole heiress of John Tahattawan, Sachem and late of Nashobah deceased; Naanishcow, alias John Thomas; Naanasquaw alias Rebeckah, wife to the said Naanishcow; Naashkinomenet, alias Solomon, eldest son of said Naanishcow and Naanasquaw, sister to the aforesaid Tahattawan; Weegrammominet alias Thomas Waban; Nackcominewock, relict of Crooked Robin; Wunnuhhew alias Sarah, wife to Neepanum alias Tom Dubelet."

This deed gave insight into the Indian bloodlines and controlling interest associated with Nashobah Plantation. All of the

Indians in the line of succession from old Tahattawan are listed, and are in a hierarchy of ranking. I will examine each in turn, using the successionship rules outlined in Shattuck's description of the Squaw Sachem of Musketaquid.

Bear in mind that there is a difference between a sachem and a sagamore. A sachem is a leader, but a sagamore is a sachem of royal blood whose sachemship was passed down through family generations. Old Tahattawan was a sagamore, a "sachem of the blood" as Eliot termed it.

The Bulkeley-Henchman deed began with Sarah-Kehonowsquaw proclaiming her right as standing at the head of succession to old Tahattawan. Kehonowsquaw was the daughter of John Tahattawan and his wife Sarah-Wunnuhhew. Sarah-Wunnuhhew was the daughter of Sagamore-John of Wamesit and therefore was of royal blood herself. This made Sarah-Kehonowsquaw the daughter of two royal lines. Wamesit was described by Gookin in the *Historical Collections of the Indians of New England* as being "an ancient and capital seat of Indians." John Tahattawan and Sarah-Wunnuhhew had a son as well, but he was only seven years old at the time of his father's death.

Troubles

Sarah-Wunnuhhew became the Squaw Sachem of Nashobah upon her husband's death around 1670, her son having been too young to rule. She remarried shortly afterward to John Owannamug, the sachem of the Praying Indian village of Okommakamesit (Marlborough), who then became the sachem of Nashobah through her. But according to Gookin, Owannamug died in July of 1674. With this, Sarah-Wunnuhhew added the sachemship of Okommakamesit to her titles.

Note 3: Okommakamesit also went by the extraordinarily

odd name of Whip Suffrage. It is unknown how the name came about, but part of the Whip Suffrage lands became the town of Marlborough under Lieutenant John Ruddock, the same man who took James Speen's gun after the siege of Quaboag. The name Marlborough was in honor of a thriving borough in John Ruddock's old English county of Wiltshire. (Sumner Chilton Powell, Puritan Village, 1963)

In June of 1681, Sarah-Wunnuhhew was referenced as "Sarah-Onnamag" petitioning to sell land in "whip suffrage the Indian plantation near Marlborough" which she inherited from her second husband Owannamug. (Massachusetts Archives, Vol. 30, Page 258a)

Note 4: John Owannamug (variants Onomog, Oonamog) of Okommakamesit is not to be confused with John Oosumog (variant Awssamug), who was the husband of Yawata, the daughter of Nanepashemet and Squaw Sachem. Owannamug died in July of 1674, and Oonsumug was named on a deed in 1680.

But it was only in title. Eliot had replaced the blood sachems of the Praying villages with civil appointees upon their deaths. For example, in Nashobah, after John Tahattawan's death the rulership was given by Eliot to Captain Josiah (Pennahannit), who was neither a sachem nor a sagamore. Further, female rulers were not part of Eliot's Puritan worldview; the Praying villages were run by men.

So although Sarah-Wunnuhhew by the traditional reckoning became the Squaw Sachem of Nashobah, the new reality under Eliot gave the rulership to Captain Josiah. The same situation was in effect in Okommakamesit; Sarah remained there for a year, and although it was unlikely that she presided as Squaw Sachem, she was leader of a contingent of Pawtucket from Wamesit who made their home with her. It also appears that after the death of Owannamug, the sachemship of Nashobah did not automatically revert to her, but went to her children.

As King Philip's War heated up in August of 1675, the Okommakamesit Praying Village was broken up by Captain Mosley in retaliation for the Indian raid on Lancaster, and Sarah returned to her childhood village of Wamesit, bringing some of her people with her.

More trouble developed in Wamesit that November, and on the 15th Sarah-Wunnuhhew's 12-year-old son—the hereditary blood-sachem of Nashobah—was killed. A bullet from a mob of revenge-minded Chelmsford men fired into a crowd of Praying Indian women and children ended his life and severely wounded Sarah-Wunnahhew. This left the sachemship of Nashobah to Sarah-Kehonowsquaw, the "daughter and sole heiress of John Tahattawan."

Even more blows were to fall in Wamesit. In fear of their lives, and with news of the Nashobah Praying Indians having been removed to Concord, the Wamesit fled into the woods and did not return until mid-December, by then in "a forlorn condition," according to Drake.

Two months later, when Captain Mosley forcefully moved the Nashobah to Deer Island on February 21 in retaliation for the Indian raids on the Eames and Shepard families, the Wamesit under Numphow and John Lyne again fled to the woods, this time heading north seeking sanctuary with Wonalancet in Canada.

This was disastrous. Not only were the few aged and infirm Wamesit that were left behind killed; but the rest wandered in the frozen woods for months, many of whom, including Numphow, dying of hunger and exposure. When they returned and surrendered in August of 1676, some were accused of bearing arms against the English and were either sold into slavery or hanged.

Where Sarah-Wunnuhhew was in all this and how she managed to survive is not known. She had been severely wounded on November 15; was she well enough by late February to take the long trek in the frozen wilds, or was she in Concord with her Nashobah kin recovering at John Hoar's workhouse, only to be marched to Deer Island a few days before the Wamesit fled north? She certainly could not have stayed behind, infirm, in Wamesit. All who did were killed shortly afterward.

All that is known is that she survived and turned up again in the historical record 1684. She would have been approximately 52 years old and had lived through many sorrows.

Sachemship and Nashobah

There is some debate whether John Tahattawan had a brother, referred to as William Nahaton. Sources differ on this, and the issue is examined in depth in Chapter 2, *Tom Dublet and Deer Island*. In light of the successionship we see in the 1686 deed, he was either not a brother, or had died by then along with his wife and any children. (Otherwise they would have been named in the deed.)

The next closest to the Nashobah sachemship was Nashobah Indian minister John Thomas (Naanishcow), who was married to old Tahattawan's daughter Rebeckah (Naanasquaw). It was through her that he gained this close proximity to the sachemship. He was followed in the list by his son Solomon (Naashkinomenet).

John Thomas hadn't simply married into royalty—he had standing in his own right. He would not have been able to marry a sagamore's daughter had he not also been of a royal line. He was the Indian minister of Nashobah and had inherited the position from his father sometime between 1665 and 1670. (He was followed in his position by James Speen.)

This was a prestigious role, and there was more to it than meets the eye. Susan L. MacCulloch said in *A Tripartite Political System among Christian Indians of Early Massachusetts*, 1966, that the Indian ministers were usually the sons of sachems. For example, James Speen was the son of Sagamore Old Speen, according to Mandell in *Behind the Frontier*. This, and Thomas' marriage to old Tahattawan's daughter, confirm that the Thomas line was a royal line as well.

The next closest to the sachemship after the John Thomas family was Thomas Waban (Weegrammominet). Thomas Waban was the son of old Tahattawan's eldest daughter, Tasunsquaw, and Waban, one of Eliot's first converts and his civil leader of Natick. According to Shattuck, Waban "was not a sachem by birth, as some have asserted, but acquired rights in the soil and assented to its sale, by virtue of his marriage into the 'royal family.'"

Note 5: Shattuck was probably incorrect about Waban, who was the leader of Natick, the first Praying Village established. Native royalty did not out-marry, but kept marriage tightly relegated between others of the same rank. Old Tahattawan was a sagamore "of the blood." It is unlikely that he would marry his eldest daughter to common blood. As well, MacCulloch asserted in her widely cited study that "in almost every [known] case" the rulers of Praying villages were sachems or sagamores. (Susan L. MacCulloch, A Tripartite Political System among Christian Indians of Early Massachusetts, 1966)

This only bears out for the original villages, however, not the later ones. Typically the first Praying villages were set up under traditional Native leadership to ease the process, but as time went on and new Praying Villages were created, or existing traditional leaders passed away, Eliot placed appointed civil leaders in their stead. It is hard to imagine that the initial Praying village in Natick could have been achieved without putting it under the leadership of an established sachem or sagamore.

Waban was not on the 1686 deed—he had died the previous year—but his son Thomas Waban was, and Thomas had royal Tahattawan blood from his mother. To be listed higher than Waban's son, John Thomas must have had royal blood of his own right by way of his father.

After Thomas Waban in the line of successionship came "Nackcominewock, relict of Crooked Robin." Robin was Petavit, "one of the late rulers of Hassanamesit who died not above three days before our coming," according to Gookin in September of 1674. Hassanamesit is Grafton, and for his wife to have been listed after his death in the successionship meant that she was of the Tahattawan bloodline in some way.

The final grantor on the deed was "Wunnuhhew alias Sarah, wife to Neepanum alias Tom Dubelet." This was Sarah Doublet, or Sarah Indian, referred to in the 1714 act of Incorporation. She was of the Wamesit royal blood and her first marriage was to John Tahattawan. She was the mother of Sarah-Kehonowsquaw.

Sarah-Wunnuhhew was listed last because her later marriages had distanced her from her connection to John Tahattawan and Nashobah's sachemship. She was distanced from the Squaw Sachemship of Nashobah when Owannamug died, and she was distanced from the Squaw Sachemship of Okommakamesit when she married Tom Dublet (Neepanum/Nepanet), of whose lineage we know little.

Again this was a situation where the royal connection was through the wife. Sarah Doublet was the grantor on the deed, not Tom Dublet. It was as Mandell pointed out: "Thomas Waban, for example, held a connection to Nashobah's Sachemship through his mother, and Thomas Dublet had a similar affiliation through his wife."

Sarah-Wunnuhhew married Tom Dublet sometime between 1681 and 1684. This is evidenced by her petition in May of 1681 to the court to sell land that formerly belonged to Owannamug. The petition reads, "Sarah Onnamag widow relicts of Onnamage." She asked to do so "for maintenance of her self and children." But in the Willard deed of 1684, Sarah was now the wife of Tom: "Thomas Dublett and Sarah his wife, Daughter of John Sagamore, all Indians of Nashoby." (She is referred to as Sarah Indian later in the deed.)

In the post-King Philip's War era, and with the passing of John Eliot in 1690 at age 86, blood sachemship became the tribal mode of governance again. With this, the traditional authority that came with successionship became a factor once more and the old ties were resurrected; Sarah-Wunnuhhew's ties to the Nashobah sachemship meant something again.

The 1686 Bulkeley-Henchman deed is like a "who's who" of the Nashobah sachemship. But the last two deeds, the 1694 Powers deed and the 1701 Whitcomb deed, have only a few Indian grantors.

The Powers deed was granted by Thomas Waban, who traced his bloodline back to old Tahattawan through his mother Tasun-squaw. The deed itself mentioned John Thomas, who had successfully challenged the sale at that time of what would become the Whitcomb deed. John Thomas was one step higher than Thomas Waban in the succession line, and was in the position to prevent that part of the sale. In 1701 it would seem that John Thomas had a change of heart and allowed his sons Solomon Thomas and John Thomas Jr. to sell to Whitcomb.

We can infer from this that Sarah-Kehonowsquaw had passed away by 1694; otherwise she as the Squaw Sachem of Nashobah would have been the grantor. We can also deduce that the sachemship was held by John Thomas Sr. after her passing. He was able to prevent Thomas Waban from selling land in 1694. In 1701 he was 84 years old, but he would have to have approved the Whitcomb sale. He certainly did not drop out of business dealings in his old age, nor was it the Indian custom to relinquish sachemship to anything but death.

In confirmation of his continued involvement in Sachemship affairs, in 1714 a confirmatory deed of the Bulkeley-Henchman purchase was issued by John Thomas Sr., John Thomas Jr., and Thomas Waban. John Thomas Sr. was 97 years old at the time.

Where was Sarah-Wunnuhhew, wife of Tom Dublet, in all this? What we know is that her marriages had distanced her from the sachemship and she was at the bottom of the successionship line in 1686. She was not named as a grantor on either the 1694 or 1701 deeds of Nashobah lands.

And yet, 13 years later in 1714, the Great and General Court of the Province of Massachusetts Bay had written into the Act of Incorporation of Littleton that "a portion thereof to be for Sarah Dublet alias Sarah Indian."

Several observations can be drawn from this. It is unlikely she would be called out by name were she not living in Nashobah.

Also, she was no doubt part of the "two or three families only remaining" living on the land set aside in 1702. Also, there were other Indians living there; we know this from the 1711 committee that went to "view the land." Finally, for her to have been singled out by name by the Court meant she must have been the most prominent or powerful Indian living there; the English preferred to deal with the sachems and sagamores or their heirs wherever possible in land dealings.

So she most likely was the most powerful Indian living there, and her power derived from her connection to the Nashobah sachemship. Her apparent rise in power would have stemmed from two things. She seems to have outlived others closer to the sachemship than she was, and second, she was of royal blood and the widow of John Tahattawan, and their children were deceased. As such, that made her John Tahattawan's heir to the English. She may have been higher up the succession line in the English view than in the Indian view.

And this is implied in the way that the set-aside is worded in the Act of Incorporation. The relevant part reads that the reservation was for the "benefit of any of the descendants of the Indian proprietors of the said plantation, that may be surviving; and Sarah Doublet, Sarah Indian." This implied that Sarah Doublet was *not* a descendant of Old Tahattawan, but had a special right of her own to be there—such as having been his son's wife.

Note 6: This 500-acre tract is one of the first Indian reservations. The earliest reservation, the Mohegan Reservation, is in Montville, Connecticut, and dates back to 1666. The Feather News on July 8, 2009, quoted the Pequots' hired archeologist, Kevin McBride, as saying it "is the earliest reservation in the United States." However, in 1666 this was not the United States but the English Colony of Connecticut.

The authority for Sarah-Wunnuhhew's lineage is from Herbert Harwood. In the *Proceedings of the Littleton Historical Society*, regarding Sarah and Tom Dublet, Harwood started with an observation based on the grantors of the 1686 Bulkeley-Henchman deed, "from which," he says, "I infer they *may* have been also descendants of old Tahattawan." He followed this with a list of various Indians who were in Nashobah and mentioned "Mr. John Sagamore" who he then said was the "father of Sarah the wife of Tom Dublet."

Harwood further gave a genealogical chart of the descendants of old Tahattawan in which he listed as the wife of John Tahattawan "Sarah, dau. Sagamore John of Wamesits, she m. 2d Oonamog."

More recent authors imply that Sarah Doublet was a great-granddaughter of old Tahattawan. John Hanson Mitchell in *Trespassing* (1998) cites an unnamed local man in this regard who did research on the Tahattawan line. I have not found any confirmation of this conclusion, but, admittedly, it is a difficult area of research.

Note 7: There is some confusion in Mitchell's Trespassing regarding Sarah Doublet. She is identified as "probably" the great-granddaughter of old Tahattawan, but later in the book she is referred to as "She, Sarah Doublet, Kehonowsquaw." However, as both Sarah Doublet and Sarah-Kehonowsquaw were signees on the 1686 Bulkeley-Henchman deed, they could not be the same person, and it's a fact that Sarah-Kehonowsquaw was the daughter of Sarah-Wunnuhhew (Doublet).

When Sarah-Wunnuhhew died sometime after September of 1736, she had outlived all the other Nashobah Indians in the successionship. Even John Thomas Sr. had passed away in 1727 in Natick at the ripe old age of 110 years. She was the only Indian living in the New Town, and at the end of her life deeded the entire tract to Jones & Jones. This tract had been set aside in 1714 for "any of the descendants of the Indian proprietors of the said plantation," so we can assume by this that there weren't any, or that Sarah bought them out.

The Indian New Town

On November 30, 1714, the Littleton town lines were officially established and the provision of 500 acres for the Indian descendants laid out. This is described in a committee report made to the General Court on December 14, 1714, as follows: "And we have laid out to the Descendants of the Indians Five hundred Acres at the South East Corner of the Plantation of Nashoba; East side, Three hundred Poles long, West side three hundred Poles, South & North ends, Two hundred and eighty Poles broad; A large white Oak marked at the North west Corner, and many Live Trees we marked at the West Side & North End, & it takes in Part of two Ponds."

Note 8: According to the Act of Incorporation, the layout of the 500 acres was done by "Cpt. Hopestill Brown, Mr. Timothy Wily & Mr. Joseph Burnap of Reading." They were also ordered to "run the line between Groton & Nashoba" to resolve the issue of who owned what, once and for all.

The two ponds are Nagog Pond and Fort Pond. The 500-acre reservation for the descendants of the Indian proprietors became known as the Indian New Town, as opposed to the old town of Nashobah Plantation times. Such landmarks as Newtown Road and Newtown Hill were named in the era of the Indian New Town.

Note 9: To quote from the Massachusetts Historical Commis-

sion's inventory of historic houses in Littleton, "Newtown Road is one of the oldest routes in Littleton, descended from a secondary branch of native trails which followed Shaker Lane and Newtown Road to Fort Pond." This path came out at Quagana Hill in the Powers Farm area, connecting the Indian village and Concord Village.

The Indian New Town was about nine-tenths of a mile square and tucked into the southeast corner of the newly incorporated English township of Nashoba, which was an irregular rectangle at the time. The easterly and southerly bounds of the Indian New Town were also the town line. These bounds as described in the December 1714 layout only make sense, and can only be located, by understanding town bounds. The town bounds at the time of the Incorporation were the bounds of the old Nashobah Plantation of the Praying Indians.

The best description of the 500-acre New Town came from the deed from Sarah Doublet to Elnathan and Ephraim Jones executed on September 24, 1736:

"Beginning at a heap of stones on Acton line about twenty rods south of Nagog pond from thence running West about seven degrees and half south by several old marks on Acton line about two hundred and eighty five rods then turning a right angle and running north about seven degrees and half west by a heap or row of stones where a pine tree marked is fallen down and taking in part of Fort Pond and so on to a white oak tree marked near Edward Wheelers house being about two hundred and eighty five rods then turning a right angle and running east about seven and a half degrees north by land belonging to Benjamin Barron and land belong to Thomas Blanchard about two hundred and eighty five rods to a heap of stones then turning a right angle and running south about seven degrees and half east by several old marks to the first mentioned corner being about two hundred and eighty five rods taking in part of Nagog Pond."

Why Here?

Why was this corner of Littleton was selected as the site of the Indian New Town? First of all, the original Court provision of 1702 required a set-aside for the Indians. It seems reasonable that wherever this set-aside established in 1702 was, it would be the same area as the official reservation of 1714. The "two or three families only remaining" noted at Incorporation would most likely have still been living in the 1702 provision area, and it is logical that this would have been rolled over into the reservation of 1714.

Another consideration is that this corner of town was the least desirable from an English agricultural perspective. It is rocky, swampy, and hilly, and much of it is lake. From an English proprietor's standpoint, it would have been the least favorable land in town for farm-lots, and they would be more inclined to let this go for the reservation than more desirable land.

Modern writers like John Hanson Mitchell (*Trespassing*, 1998) have conjectured that this area between Nagog Pond and Fort Pond was sacred and that the Indians held onto it until the bitter end. I also believe that the Nashobah area was sacred, a center of shamanic practice and vision-quest in late Woodland and Early Contact times, and have written on it extensively.

Note 10: Mitchell says in Trespassing: "Historians of the native Americans of this period believe that the last tracts of land the Indians would surrender were those that held spiritual significance for them. Hunting grounds, even agricultural land, may have been sold off or traded, but the last to go would have been those areas that were sacred."

However, the truth of the matter is that when the post-Deer Island Nashobah Indians sold this part of the plantation to Bulkeley and Henchman in 1686, it was one of the first pieces sold, not one of the last. Indeed, they not only sold the site of the old village in this transaction, but also the area that some people, including both Mitchell and I, believe was the heart of the spiritually significant zone.

It is intriguing that the 1702 provision required the petitioners to "agree with the Indians yet remaining upon ye place for a convenient settlement." This implied that the Indians were to be given a choice of location, and they chose the old village site as evidenced by the placement of the 1714 reservation. This can also be taken as part of the argument that they chose as their own the sacred part of the old vision-quest area. This echoes the original selection of the area in 1654 by old Tahattawan, who was given the choice of here he wanted the new Praying village to be; he chose the area that became Nashobah Plantation.

When given the option, the Indians chose Nashobah in 1654, and given the choice in Nashobah in 1702, they chose the New Town area. According to this theory, this chain of choice narrowed down the sacred vision-quest center to the Indian New Town.

But others, like James Mavor and Byron Dix in *Manitou* (1989), who have studied the Nashoba area in view of what they call the "sacred landscape of New England native civilization," feel the heart of the vision-quest activity was actually at the esker at Beaver Brook, then part of Nashobah Plantation, now part of Boxborough. Of this they say, "We believe that the shaman-preachers of Nashoba used the praying villages to maintain the Indian communication links, the sacred landscape and the stone and earthen structures in the midst of encroaching white colonists. We believe that central to their world was the Boxborough esker."

There are certainly fascinating features at Muddy Pond at the esker, and what catches the eye here in terms of holding onto the sacred part of the land the longest is the fact that this part of Nashobah was indeed the very last part sold, going to Josiah Whitcomb in 1701. Walter Powers had wanted to buy this in 1694 but was prevented from doing so by an old Indian, John Thomas, who successfully prevented the purchase, as discussed in the deed itself: the "Westerly quarter part of ye plantation is yet in possession of ye Indians being challenged by John Thomas Indian." (This was eventually sold by his sons in 1701 to Josiah Whitcomb.)

The section that Walter Powers bought also included the entirety of Tophet Chasm and Tophet Swamp at Oak Hill, a locale that can be strongly associated with Indian ceremony and powwowing.

The question of vision-quest sites aside, it is my opinion that the New Town site was chosen because this was where the old village was, and it was an area not so valuable to the English. As well, it came out of the Bulkeley-Henchman deed and Thomas Henchman was well-known as a friend of the Indians and was respected among them. He, more than any other deed-holder, was more likely to provide the 1702 set-aside for the Indians out of his tract.

I think more than anything, the few Indians who had continued to stay on, or came and went with the planting and gathering seasons, were for the most part living in Speen's End where the original village had been and the fort and burials were located.

Sarah Doublet's Cave

There is an oral tradition that Sarah Doublet lived in a cave somewhere in what is now the Sarah Doublet Forest. The problem with this is there is no known cave in the area—indeed, I had walked the land hundreds of times since the late 1970s and did not believe there was even the possibility of a cave up there. Other people I knew wove various theories about the cave, that it was actually a lean-to of branches up against a large boulder on the hilltop, for example. This all changed one spring morning in the early 1990s when I was out for a walk in the Sarah Doublet Forest.

I heard the approach of a large, loud family complete with several rambunctious dogs, and not feeling quite sociable that morning, I ducked down behind a large tree growing on a slope next to a stone wall and a mound of ledge-rock, and stooped between the tree and the ledge. In so doing, I noticed that there was a small opening between the ledge and tree next to me. The opening was at ground level about five inches high and eight inches wide. Peering in, I could see into a large dark underground space.

After examination with a flashlight the space proved to be an underground chamber. The tree had grown up in front of the opening and blocked it entirely except for the small "window" still open at its base. I would never have seen it had I not been hunkered down next to it. Indeed, I had actually walked over the roof slab hundreds of times over the years.

Note 11: The tree blocking the entrance is a scarlet oak, and based in its diameter at chest height it is approximately 66 years old. According to the International Society of Arboriculture, a tree's age can be approximated by multiplying the diameter by a "growth factor" in scarlet oaks of four. This age value is based on averages, and a number of factors can impact it such as climate, soil, and tree density. To obtain an exact age, the tree would need to be core-sampled with an increment borer.

The far end of the chamber was constructed with fieldstone, and I was able to remove some of these and crawl into the chamber. I found the size to about eight feet long, five feet wide at its widest point, and about 14 inches high inside. Probing revealed that the chamber had filled with 12 to 14 inches of forest detritus, giving a headspace at one time of almost three feet.

The chamber had been constructed of ledge slabs. A ledge slab had been pulled away from its parent rock by about four feet, leaving a space between them of about eight feet long, four to five feet wide, and two and half to three feet deep. Over this another ledge slab had been pulled away from the parent rock to cover the cavity. This could not have happened naturally as the top slab would have fallen into the cavity rather than cover it. The back end of the cavity was then carefully blocked up with fieldstone.

I feel strongly this is the "cave" associated with Sarah Doublet. However, it is not a structure one could live in, and so would not have been her dwelling—she would have lived in a wigwam—but what the tradition of her and the cave actually does is *associate the chamber with Indian activity*: It indicates this might have been an underground place used by Indians of at least the Nashobah Plantation era.

Mavor and Dix in *Manitou* considered these underground chambers to be "vision-quest" sites, similar in placement and use to the kivas in the American Southwest. In this respect, the Sarah Doublet Forest chamber need not be dwelling-sized, but only large enough to comfortably contain a person for a period of fasting and meditation.

The chamber is significantly situated under a dome of ledge that is the highest point of the Sarah Doublet Forest. The entrance of the chamber faces southeast in the general direction of the Winter Solstice Sunrise. The entire hill is only recently grown over with scrub oak and Scotch pines; before this it was open and heath-like. Indeed, it was still open enough that as recently as the early 1980s, I can recall being able at to watch at sunset both the moon rising on the eastern horizon and the setting sun in the west as it slipped below the low hills.

There is also a stone row that runs over the top of the chamber. Interestingly, at the point it runs over the chamber dome and in several dozen feet in either direction, it is composed of exceedingly large slabs of rock. It also follows the contours of the ledge rather than running in a straight line, and makes bridges over gaps in the ledge-face. However, if followed farther in either direction, the row-rocks diminish into regular Colonial-style stonework and follow regular Colonial-style straight lines.

The chamber itself is a cavity in a granite ledge covered with a granite slab. Considering that granite is a radon-bearing rock, and radon gas awareness is a health issue in Littleton, it's possible that radon poisoning—or more precisely, its possible effects—may have in some way contributed to vision-quest experiences in the small Sarah Doublet Chamber.

Indeed, Indians were not the only ones who have found the hill spiritually attractive. It's not uncommon to stumble upon a quiet soul perched upon a rock in mediation, and occasionally monks from Westford's Wat Buddhabhavana Buddhist Meditation Center. And perhaps most significantly from the perspective of Indian ceremonies, modern Neo-Pagans constructed a stone circle at the dome and worshipped Lady Nature there for years.

CHAPTER 4
THE LAST INDIAN

THE INDIANS WERE AN ISSUE TO THE PURITANS; THE ISSUE WAS LAND and religion, but primarily land. Although the King of England proclaimed he owned all of New England by the virtue of it having been "discovered" by an Englishman (and claimed as such for the Crown), it was another matter to get the Indians to agree to any such sweeping declaration. In fact, they didn't. The English Puritans were in the position of having to buy the land they wanted from the Indians even though it was supposedly owned by the Crown. The Crown could grant them all the land it wanted, and did, but unless there was a concurrent backroom sale from the Indians, nothing actually changed hands.

It didn't help that the Indians weren't God-fearing Calvinists. Rather, according to the leading Boston Puritan minister Cotton Mather, they were *Heathens*. And they didn't wear clothes the way the English did, which affronted them, and which they took as a sign of their spiritual benightedness.

Note 1: Native "nakedness" was of no small issue to the Puritans. According to Jill Lepore in her 1998 Name of War, the "Eng-

lish colonists perceived bodily nakedness as signaling both cultural and spiritual depravity, marking the Indians as doubly lacking. Thus the move 'from Barbarism to Civilitie' could only be accomplished by the Indians' 'forsaking their filthy nakedness.'" (Lepore is referencing a letter written by dissident New World theologian, Roger Williams, composed sometime between 1631 and 1683.)

Clothes, to the English, were a marker of civilization. Lepore went on to say that the Indians were "keenly aware that the English dressed differently: the Narragansett word for European is 'Wautacondug,' or literally, 'Coatman,' deriving from 'Wautacome,' meaning 'one that wears clothes.'" (Lepore is again referencing Williams, this time his book "A Key in to the Language of America.")

The Puritans were religious dissenters from England and they had come to the New World to build a New Jerusalem, which they spoke of as a Shining City on a Hill. This was to be God's country, under God's will, filled with God's people, doing God's work, for the glory of God.

David Cody in *Puritanism in New England* (1988) elaborates: "Their isolation in the New World, their introversion, the harshness and dangers of their new existence, their sense that they were a new Chosen People of God destined to found a New Jerusalem – a New City of God in the midst of the wilderness."

Note 2: Regarding the Puritans' New Jerusalem, Paul Boyer of PBS/Frontline comments: "There's the vision of the New Jerusalem, the city on a hill. This is the chosen land for the new Zion. Increase Mather, the father of Cotton Mather, certainly expresses this theme in his sermons." (Paul Boyer, The Puritans, PBS/Frontline.)

But these "heathen" Indians were everywhere, and they had all the land—a bigger challenge to God's design there could not be. Something had to give as both sides pushed against each other with no mutual social, cultural, linguistic, or religious common ground. What ended up giving were the Indians, but not without a fight. This fight, which was more a long defeat spread over any number of heartbreaking years, can be seen in microcosm in King Philip's War of 1675-1676.

This is an oversimplification of the situation—a situation that much has been written about and debated over since the Puritans arrived almost 400 years ago. My task in this chapter is not to recount this big-picture history, or even to try and make full sense of it, but to tell instead of the Praying Indians in Nashobah Plantation and what happened to them, which was not unlike the final result of what happened to the wolves and rattlesnakes—they disappeared, at least as a visible culture.

In October of 1659, when John Eliot, apostle to the Indians, petitioned the court for surveyor Johnathan Danforth to lay out Nashobah, he also included a clause that Indians "be allowed no power to sell their land." But it is doubtful this clause of the petition was granted; I have found nothing to indicate it became an act of the General Court. (*Massachusetts Archives*, Vol. 30, Page 81)

The reason Eliot sought this was that the Indians and the English had thoroughly different conceptions of land use. The English had a system of private ownership, but the Indians used the land communally under a sachem who had authority over a territory as a whole. When selling land, the Indians saw it as something like a transfer of sachemship over the area, not as it becoming private property they would no longer be allowed on or allowed to use. They still expected to be able to use the land under the new "English sachem."

With this mismatch of understanding, it was easy for the Indians to sell off their land, not realizing they were also selling off their homes and livelihood—the result of which was disastrous. It was for this reason that Eliot wanted to make sure that the new Praying villages would remain stable communities and would not get sold out from under them. He wanted to make sure these new Indian towns had a future.

Note 3: There was at least one law on the books against direct land transactions between the English and Indians, but it had to do with title issues, not protecting the Indians. The legal method at the time was to go through the General Court, not transfer land directly between parties.

After King Philip's War, the Nashobah spent some time in Charlestown and then in Concord in the autumn of 1676, many as servants of the English, sheltering against the Mohawk threat that followed the end of the war. There were a good 50 Nashobah, and they had survived Deer Island more intact than most villages.

But even after the threat of the Mohawks subsided again later that year, and with an agreement between them and the English reached, the Nashobah faded back to Natick as most of the other Praying Indians had begun doing in the fall of 1677, and made a collective community there. They did not try to reestablish Nashobah Plantation as a residence, although they did plant there. The 10 or so men of the village were not enough to man a fort in case the Mohawk started up again (which they did). But in Natick (as well as Punkapoag), there were enough men to defend a fort, and both towns rebuilt theirs.

Note 4: This consolidation in Natick, which ensued over the years as other Massachusett Nation Praying plantations dwindled, resulted in a regrouping as the Praying Indians of Natick-Ponkapoag-(Nashobah) under one Massachusett sachem.

. . .

Further, in May of 1677 the General Court had confined all the Praying Indians to the villages of Natick, Punkapoag, Hassanamesit, and Wamesit according to Daniel Mandell in *Behind the Frontier* (1996). This was not enforced, but it served as another determent to the resettlement of Nashobah Plantation.

The English appetite for land had grown strong, and here was a great big tract of open land—the last of its kind in the area—and the English wanted it. In 1684 Nashobah was but "inhabited by a small parcel of Indians, but for many years hath been deserted, all dead except some few yet are dispersed." And it is true—Nashobah had been deserted as a functioning village since November of 1675, when they were taken to Concord.

Not surprisingly, the English neighbors of Nashobah Plantation began eyeing the property. According to Harwood in his *Historical Sketch of Littleton*, "the English had already moved into the deserted plantation and settled there with no real right. Some had bought land from the Indians, but this was done illegally as it had been expressly forbidden by the General Court" of Massachusetts Bay Colony.

Note 5: Some had indeed bought land illegally from the Indians, as early as 1682, but there is no evidence that the Nashobah-owned portions of the Plantation had been seized and settled by the English. Rather, we see settlement following purchase, albeit illegal purchase. But this is not to say that squatting or trespassing did not occur.

The first attempt to gain control of Nashobah Plantation was on May 19, 1680, "When 23 inhabitants of Concord petitioned the General Court that the lands belonging to those Indians might be granted to them," as related by Lemuel Shattuck in his 1835 *History of the Town of Concord*.

But the bid was rejected because there were "debts due from the country which might be provided for by the sale of the land, if the Indians have no right or have deserted the place."

Rather than go through the courts, the next attempt went directly to the Indians, who consented to sell. The first piece of Nashobah Plantation the Praying Indians sold was a small slice next to Groton, which went to Peleg Lawrence and Robert Robbins, both of Groton, in about 1682. It was about a half a mile wide and two miles long.

Following this, in 1686 the Nashobahs sold the entire northeast half of the plantation to Peter Bulkeley of Concord and Major Thomas Henchman of Chelmsford. Henchman had served as a lieutenant in King Philip's War and was a friend of the Wamesit Praying Indians.

This purchase included the Praying Indian village itself, Speen's field, the fort on the hillside above Fort Pond, and the burial grounds near the lake.

Eight years later in 1694, the Indians sold half of the remaining land to their longtime neighbor in Concord Village, Walter Powers. This constituted one-quarter of the original Nashobah Plantation. The last of Nashobah Plantation, the westernmost quarter, was sold in 1701 to Josiah Whitcomb of Lancaster.

But there were problems with these sales. They were all done outside the court, and so were "clandestine and illegal." In 1701 a new bill had been passed into law to make void and null any and all clandestine and illegal purchases from the Indians, retroactive to 1633. (*Massachusetts Archives* Vol. 30, Pages 348-9; *Massachusetts Archives* Vol. 30, Pages 474-5) However, this did not revert the property back to the Indians; it simply meant the English deed holders had to take the voided deeds to court and have them reinstated (for a fee) through the proper procedures.

With the 1701 deed to Josiah Whitcomb, Nashobah Plantation was all gone. Unlike the wolves and rattlesnakes, the Indians of Nashobah Plantation were not hunted out. Rather, they were slowly bought out. It was their land that the local Englishmen wanted. Unlike the Wampanoag and Nipmucks under King Philip, the Praying Indians in Nashobah had never ravaged their English neighbors. As such, neither had they been hunted down and killed nor sold into slavery, unlike Philip and his allies.

This is not to say that their quarantine on Deer Island had been humane—it wasn't—or that they had been treated well during the war or afterward. They weren't. Rather, the English were still going through the motions of purchase and sale, rather than just taking the vacated land.

The Governor's Council had sent the Praying Indians to Deer Island ostensibly for their own protection. They felt that not only the English but also King Philp's Indians would attack them if they were not secluded somewhere out of reach of both. The main issue with Deer Island may well not be that it was done, or done for a bad reason, but that it was done badly.

The ministers, particularly Eliot, saw the Praying Indians as younger brothers or servants of the English, and many of them were integrated as servants in Concord and elsewhere after being retrieved from Deer Island. Eliot had always maintained that that Anglicizing the Indians was a necessity to successfully Christianizing them.

Edward Randolph had this in mind as well when he decried the loss of Indian life in King Philip's War in his investigation and report to King James II: "And upwards of 300 Indian men women, and children destroyed, who if well managed would have been very serviceable to the English, which makes all manner of labour dear." It was not their loss of life, but the loss of potential service to the English that he found wasteful.

Many Praying Indians had gone into service, and the trend would continue. In the May 1677 order that all Praying Indians be confined to Natick, Punkapoag, Hassanamesit, and Wamesit, the one exception was "servants and apprentices," according to Mandell.

With the final sale in 1701, the English possessed all of Nashobah Plantation. They could now petition to incorporate a town and sell farm-plots as the proprietors. But they had two problems: They held the land illegally, and not all the Indians were gone.

They tackled the first problem by petitioning the General Court in October of 1702 for a confirmation of their Indian deeds, seeking to make them legal. They had to. A 1701 law voided any and all "clandestine and illegal purchases from the Indians."

In this petition Henchman, Powers, and Whitcomb, and the lawyer acting on behalf of the estate of Bulkeley stated that the Nashobah Indians had "removed themselves and families to Natick and having no occasion for their lands at Nashoby [Nashobah] ... and are reduced to very few."

The second problem was heightened by the petition of James Speen in January 1701 over some lost guns. The Speen petition, wherein he gave his name and residence as "I James Speen Indian of *Nashobah,*" was made some months prior to the Henchman, Powers, and Whitcomb petition.

Whatever Henchman, Powers, and Whitcomb, and Bulkeley's lawyer may have wanted the Great and General Court of the Province of Massachusetts Bay to think about Nashobah being deserted of Indians; at least some such as Speen were still in town living at the old village by the pond.

The General Court was not buying it that the plantation was deserted, and only confirmed the deeds provisionally—that the petitioners "agree with ye Indians yet remain upon ye place for a convenient settlement." That is, they had to make room for the Indians who remained if they wanted their deeds to be made legal.

The archive abstract is even blunter: "House resolved to grant the petition provided a place was maintained for those Indians who wished to stay."

From 1702 to 1711 there is no more known about it, but presumably some sort of arrangement had been worked out.

In 1711 a petition was introduced to the Great and General Court to incorporate a new township out of the Nashobah lands comprised of the Henchman, Bulkeley, Powers, and Whitcomb parcels. This was read in the House of Representatives and approved but not acted on by the Council until two years later. The petitioners noted that Nashobah was *"practically deserted by the Indians."* (Italics mine.)

The response from the House to the petition indicates that it wasn't as deserted as described; there were still *"two or three families only remaining."* (Italics mine.)

Note 6: A family was a group like a tribe or band; it did not always mean a family unit, but a small grouping of Indians: "Larger groups are known as tribes and smaller ones are referred to as bands, and even smaller groups are known as Families." (Indian vs. English Views Regarding Rights to the Land, Southern Essex District Registry of Deeds, www.salemdeeds.com)

When the new English township of Nashoba was incorporated in 1714, the Act of Incorporation included a reservation for the Indians that remained. This was the formalization of the "convenient settlement" ordered by the General Court in 1702 as the provision of legalizing their Indian deeds.

The bounds of the town were formalized at the same time, and within this document is given the size and location of the land set aside "for the descendants of the Indians."

This reservation was called the Indian New Town (as opposed to the old town of Nashobah Plantation), which is where the local names Newtown Road and Newtown Hill come from. The location was a 500-acre square set in the southeast corner of the new English township of Nashoba. It was created out of the Bulkeley-Henchman purchase of 1686 and comprised one-sixth of the tract they purchased.

The site of the reservation seems to have been chosen for several reasons. First, it is tucked in a corner of the town out of the way. Second, it is some of the least farmable land, being mostly pond, swamp, and rocky hill and therefore less valuable to the proprietors as saleable farm-lots. Third and most important, it was the site of the old Praying Indian village in Speen's End, and had been the heart of Tahattawan's *Nashope*.

For those reasons, it is likely that the area had been the unofficial set-aside since the court order of 1702; the incorporation of 1714 simply made it official.

I think more than anything, the few Indians who had continued to stay on, or came and went with the seasons, were for the most part living in Speen's End where the original village had been and the burial grounds were located.

These few Praying Indians and their descendants—two or three families—had most likely been doing so since they got back from Deer Island, regardless of what had been sold. They simply stayed on, seasonally at times, and were still there 26 years later in 1702 when the Court ordered that provisions be made for them.

The Praying village of Nashobah Plantation had only thrived for 22 years, and for several of those had been deserted during the Mohawk wars. After King Philip's War it was mostly deserted, and 25 years later, by 1701, it had been sold entirely to the English. But the court-ordered provision of 1702 gave the Indians standing and right to a small area of their own again, and a dwindling few would remain there until Sarah Doublet's death around 1736, some 35 years later.

There are only a few names we can associate with these last dwindling years.

Thomas Dublet

Tom Dublet (Neepanum/Nepanet) was a Praying Indian who lived in Littleton after the plantation of Nashobah was sold in its entirety between 1682 and 1701. Like James Speen, where he lived had been sold early on in 1686 to Bulkeley and Henchman. Tom's name shows up on the deed as a seller. He came and went like the other Praying Indians of the time, but lived there enough that he was remembered and stories were told about him over the years, keeping his memory alive.

He was the husband of Sarah Doublet (Wunnuhhew), also called Sarah Indian, who was the aged daughter of Sagamore-John of Wamesit.

Note 7: Tom's name is best known to history with the "Dublet" spelling, and Sarah with the spelling "Doublet." It is the same name, but I keep the historical convention of the two spellings so it best matches the old records. The spelling "Dublitt" surfaces as well in the old documents.

Tom lived in a hut near his weir on Beaver Brook. In the *Proceedings of the Littleton Historical Society,* Harwood said of Joel Proctor that he "related traditions of Tom Dublet, saying that his hut was located near [his] house, and just across the street, that he was a good and tractable Indian, always friendly to white people provided they did not disturb him or fish in his hole, a short distance down the brook." Joel Proctor's house was on Great Road on the left, just past Beaver Brook going west to Groton.

Tom's weir on Beaver Brook was three miles from Speen's End and not in the Indian New Town reservation. It's not known if Tom continued to live at the weir or vacated it for the reservation, but the Proctor account does make it sound like he was at Beaver Brook after the English bought and built there.

Was this a window on the Indian worldview of land-use? Had Tom sold the land in the 1686 deed to Bulkeley and Henchman, but to him at least, not sold his right to use the land? According to Daniel Mandell in *Behind the Frontier,* the pre-Contact ethos was that "people could claim only the products of the land, not the land itself," after all. This land-use philosophy remained strong in Indian enclaves, according to Mandell. Nashobah was one such enclave.

Note 8: The Proctor account is family tradition passed down through the generations. The first Littleton Proctor, according to the reminiscences of Joel Proctor (1805-1895), was Peter Proctor, who Joel said was living on the north side of Beaver Brook by 1701. His brother Robert Proctor had the house sometime around 1721-23, and his son Nathaniel Proctor was Joel's grandfather. It is conceivable that Tom Dublet was alive in 1701 and lived across what is now Great Road at the hut and weir on Beaver Brook. (Information of Joel Proctor Aged 89 Years, April 19, 1894, Littleton Historical Society)

Tom Dublet had been quite politically involved in his later years in land issues. Between 1681 and 1685 he was part of petitions for compensation for lands in the "Nipmuck Country," which were followed by petitions protesting against fellow Indians selling land.

After his participation in selling half of Nashobah Plantation to Bulkeley and Henchman in 1686, Tom Dublet is not heard from again in the old documents.

James Speen

Alcoholism took its effect on the Indians, as well. Daniel Mandell in *Behind the Frontier*, 1996, says that the aftermath of King Philip's War "raised the Indians' use of liquor to a new level of desperation and bitterness. Drinking clearly became an addicting escape from a sense of dependence and helplessness."

The Rev. Daniel Bondet of the Huguenot village of New Oxford wrote on July 6, 1691 that "The rum is always sold to them without order and measure ... The 26th of last month there was about twenty Indians so furious by drunkenness that they fought like bears, and fell upon one ... who is appointed for preaching the gospel amongst them; he had been so much disfigured by his wounds that there is no hope of his recovery." (George Fisher Daniels, *Huguenots in the Nipmuck Country*, 1879)

By 1720, Cotton Mather lamented that rum had become a "River of Death" for the Indians, and sadly, it also caught James Speen in its sway.

James Speen had been "among the first to that prayed to god at Nonantum," where Eliot first began preaching to the Indians in October of 1647. In 1650, the Praying Indian village of Natick was created out of his family lands there, free of charge, according to Drake in *The Book of the Indians*, 1841.

He was of a royal line, the eldest son of sagamore Old Speen. He held some 16,000 acres in his own right, of which he gifted 2,000 to the new Praying Indian Village of Natick. His brothers were John, Robin, Anthony, and Thomas.

Speen was also a Praying Indian minister in both Nashobah and Pakachoog, had fought in King Philip's War for the English, survived Deer Island, and had given his family name to areas in both Nashobah and Natick; nonetheless, he "died a drunkard; having been some time before discarded from the church at Natick," said Drake. His soul had borne many griefs.

Note 9: As related in Chapter 3, Sarah Doublet's Indian New Town, Susan MacCulloch said that Praying Indian ministers were typically the sons of sachems and sagamores, which James Speen certainly was. (Susan L. MacCulloch, A Tripartite Political System among Christian Indians of Early Massachusetts, 1966)

It's likely that he made his home again in Nashobah at Fort Pond after he was cast off from the church at Natick, and his petition of 1701 where he gives his residence as "of Nashobah" is reflective of this. He was already elderly at this time, having been recorded as "old Speen" 20 years earlier in an entry in the *Massachusetts Archives*. Nashobah had been sold and the Fort Pond area passed out of Indian hands in 1686 at around the same time, yet he was there, and his name was associated with the northern end of the pond where the village had once stood and the apple trees grew.

His wife Hannah lived on, a widow, and we read of her in 1742, petitioning the court to sell some of her land to support her family. The petition was granted. (*Massachusetts Archives*, Vol. 31, Page 391)

Note 10: The 1742 petition would indicate that he married Hannah when he was old and she was young. James also had a wife, Elizabeth Speen in 1684, as seen in a confirmatory deed of that year to the town of Concord. It's also possible that Hannah was married to a different James Speen.

John Thomas

John Thomas (Naanishcow) did not actually live out his final years in Nashobah, but he is notable for his longevity and connection to Nashobah Planation and its sachemship. He was of a royal line, most likely born sometime around 1617, and married old Tahattawan's daughter Rebeckah (Naanasquaw) and had at least two sons, John Jr. and Solomon. Gookin related in the *Historical Collections of the Indians of New England* that in 1674 John Thomas was the Praying Indian minister of Nashobah, a position often held by the sons of sachems.

John was born early enough and lived long enough to have

experienced every disaster that befell the Indians of Massachusetts—from the Tarratine wars to the plagues to the arrival of the English, to King Philip's War and the disintegration and subsumption of Indian culture that followed. He is said to have died in 1727 in Natick, at the amazing age of 110 years.

Sarah Doublet

As time wore on, all the Indians of Nashobah died off one by one, but the last Indian, Sarah (Wunnuhhew) Doublet, was still there in the early 1730s. She was of powerful lineage, although there was no one to know anymore. She was the daughter of a sagamore, which means she was of royal blood, and she had been married to John Tahattawan, the son of old Tahattawan, another sagamore. Her second husband, Owannamug, was the sachem of Okommakamesit (Marlborough).

When Sarah-Kehonowsquaw, the daughter of Sarah-Wunnuhhew and John Tahattawan died between 1686 and 1694, the sachemship of Nashobah fell to John Thomas in title if not in deed. When he passed away, the sachemship came back to Sarah Doublet 57 years after she first had it as the widow of John Tahattawan.

Note 11: Sarah was due the title when she was widowed but did not receive it. Eliot stepped in and appointed Captain Josiah (Pennahannit) in her stead as part of the Colonial effort to replace Native hereditary rulership with English civil appointments.

She was still powerful in her own right and was mentioned by name in the town's Act of Incorporation in a provision that set aside the Indian New Town for her. The provision reads: "A proportion thereof to be for Sarah Dublet, alias Sarah Indian."

An echo of Sarah and her husband Tom may possibly be heard in a Blanchard family story. Deacon James Parker, who lived at the Whitney-Hoar house at 564 Newtown Road, related a family story in the Boston Globe Thanksgiving Day issue of 1897. He recalled that his "grandmother used to tell us of the old Indian chief and squaw who lingered in the forest here long after their companions had departed, and used to come to this door for a share that was always cheerfully given."

Parker's grandmother was Hannah Hoar, born in 1786, and who grew up in the house and married Calvin Blanchard Jr. in 1803. She and Calvin purchased the home from her father Samuel Hoar Jr. in 1812. It would not be out of the question for Nashobah Indians to be in the area at this time; there is record of them at Fort Pond seasonally as late as 1817.

The Whitney-Hoar house is one of the oldest houses in town and had a tradition of Indian visits. The house is less than a mile from Speen's End, and the various Whitney, Hoar, Blanchard, and Parker families had been living in close contact to both the Nashoba Plantation and later the Indian New Town from at least 1704.

While there is no reason to doubt that Hannah had been part of the tradition at that house of sharing food with the local Indians, the story of an "old Indian chief and squaw who lingered in the forest here long after their companions had departed" sounds less a firsthand account, and more like a family remembrance of Sarah and Tom, distant echo though it is.

Benjamin Hoar, who purchased the house in 1719, would certainly have known Sarah and her husband Tom if he were still alive. Sarah, at least, is known to have lingered in the forest here long after her companions had departed. When John Thomas died, the sachemship would have passed to Sarah and on to Tom if he were still alive. But since only Sarah was mentioned in the 1714 Indian New Town, Tom most likely had passed on by then.

I am guessing this is the origin of the Blanchard and Hoar family tradition of the "old Indian chief and squaw" which originated with Hannah Hoar's grandparents, Benjamin and Esther Hoar.

It is unknown what happened to Tom, but Sarah lived to an old age. She had at least two children, one of whom was 12 years old in 1675. If Sarah had him when she was 18, she would have been 91 years old in 1736 when she deeded the last of Nashobah to Elnathan and Ephraim Jones of Acton. It is not known when she passed away, only that it was after September of 1736. For all we know, she lived on for years.

Shattuck posited what happened in her twilight years: "Sarah Doublet, an Indian ... being then old and blind, and committed to the care of Samuel Jones of Concord. She then petitioned for liberty to sell it to pay her maintenance."

Note 12: In Samuel Smith's papers we find the above Shattuck quote with the date 1734 prefixed to it: "In 1734 old and blind she was committed to care of Samuel Jones of Concord." I am not a big fan of Smith's work—it is sloppy and he does not cite sources; however, the 1734 date does fit with the timeline and he has the other facts correct: Sarah was indeed under the care of Samuel (Jr.), and the Jones Tavern where Samuel lived in 1734 was not yet incorporated as the Town of Acton, but known as Concord New Grant.

As humanitarian as the Jones' care for Sarah sounds, this was often a way to gain control of Indian-held lands that could not otherwise be sold. In instances where medical debts arose, however, the sales were allowed by the courts. According to Mandell, "An increasing number of Natick Indians suffered from debts due to medical care." For instance, in 1729 Charles and Alice Watnam received permission to sell 20 acres to meet debts arising from their long illness. Jacob Chalcom of Natick sold 37 acres in 1730 to pay medical bills, and in 1737 Thomas Pegan Jr. sold land to pay medical bills, as related by Mandell.

The Jones family of Concord, in what is now West Acton, had been taking care of Sarah. Samuel Minot Jones of Concord had five sons, three of whom were Samuel, Nathanial, and Ephraim. Samuel Jr. was caring for Sarah at his house, better known as the Jones Tavern in Acton, which still stands at 128 Main Street. It was built in 1732 by Samuel Jones Jr., according to the Iron Work Farm website, and did not become a tavern until 1750.

Note 13: Local residents have recounted to me how in years past, in tours of the Jones Tavern, one of the upper rooms was described as having been where Sarah Doublet lived.

It was Samuel's brother Ephraim and his brother Nathanial's son Elnathan, who put up the money to buy the old reservation from Sarah, ostensibly so she could pay Samuel for her "maintenance," as Shattuck put it.

But according to John Hanson Mitchell in *Trespassing* (1998), the Joneses were apparently angling for water management rights for their mill, now known as Iron Work Farm.

Mitchell explains the situation: "The story of her end is that the two Jones cousins who had built the mills down at the Great Falls wanted more land to the northeast to manage the water that fed the stream that powered the mill." It was Sarah "who held the legal title to the lands the Joneses were interested in."

Note 14: Mitchell called Samuel and Ephraim Jones cousins when in actuality they were brothers.

The mill was powered by Fort Pond Brook just below where it was joined by Guggins Brook. Fort Pond Brook had its source at Fort Pond, and it was this source they apparently wished to control. However, Fort Pond Brook exits the pond outside of the area that the Jones family bought from Sarah. Unless they already owned the Fort Pond outlet, I don't see how owning the upper half of the pond had any impact as far as water-rights and water-management was concerned.

Note 15: According to A Brief History of Acton, "Guggins Brook which enters Fort Pond in West Acton was originally Gookin's Brook," named after Daniel Gookin, who was granted land here in 1668, in what is now the Guggins Brook Conservation Area. (A Brief History of Acton, 1974, Acton Historical Society) Guggins Brook has its source in Boxborough in the southeast corner of the old Nashobah Plantation.

Note 16: The original owner of Fort Pond Brook was Jonathan Prescott, who owned the southern and westerly sides. He purchased this directly from the Littleton proprietors in the first few years of the town.

The Joneses may have been genuinely caring people, but they most likely had more than one thing in mind when they took Sarah in.

Sarah's petition to sell was approved, and Harwood said in the *Proceedings of the Littleton Historical Society*, 1896, that "By authority of the Legislature, given in 1735, Sarah Doublet, otherwise called Sarah Indian, relict of Thomas, sold this reservation to Elnathan and Ephraim Jones."

Note 17: I have been unable as yet to locate the 1735 Act that allowed Sarah to sell the Indian New Town. Why this is important, is that Sarah was not actually the last Nashobah Praying Indian and as such did not have right to sell. The 1714 Act of Incorporation of Littleton specifically reads: "that five hundred acres of land be reserved and laid out for the benefit of any of the descendants of the Indian proprietors of the said plantation, that may be surviving; a portion thereof to be for Sarah Dublet alias Sarah Indian." But there were other descendants—notably the Thomas line—though not living in the Indian New Town at that time, but having previously removed to Natick. I'm curious how the Legislative Act of 1735 accounted for this.

The actual deed of September 24, 1736, runs as follows: "I Sarah Doublett alias Sarah Indian of Concord ... relict widow of Thomas Doublett deceased (having the consent and approbation of the Great and General Court) do herby for in consideration of the sun of five hundred pounds in bills of credit to me paid for my benefit and advantage secured by Elnathan and Ephraim Jones of Concord..."

I've often wondered where she was buried. Did they bring her back to the old Praying Indian burial ground in Speen's End? I'd like to think so.

Hennessy

One of the last mentions of Indians in Littleton came from Harwood, who related that "It must be remembered that the oldest Indians lived in Nashobah from 1646 and earlier to 1675, that a very few returned and Sarah Dublet was the last one, old and feeble, when the Indian farm was sold in 1736. Therefore no Indians lived here of right after that date. It is certain, however, that Indians were here at times until about the beginning of the present century [early 1800s]. Elbridge Marshall remembers a tall Indian named Hennessy or Henderson who used to come and go, and lived near the pond."

Harwood went on to say that "Others now living or recently deceased remembered Indians, or had seen their ovens and traces of huts near the pond, on the 'island' as we call the hard land surrounded by water and swamp, and on or near the flat ledge where the mountain cranberry grows, but it must be remembered that these later Indians were squatters, who came and went by sufferance, and I believe I can suggest a good reason why they camped on the island near the pond. Their ancient burying-ground was there – somewhere."

This is accurate. Harwood is referencing events from the early 1800s, and this is corroborated by an Indian basket on display at the Littleton Historical Society. The basket was bought by Samuel Conant and was "made by the Nashoba Indians at Fort Pond about 1817." It is clear from this there was an Indian presence at the pond. Based on Native habits of the era I suspect they regularly arrived for the summer and left in the fall, which is the type of itinerancy identified by Harwood when he described them camping at the pond for a while and then moving on.

Elbridge was born in 1816, so I would assume this remembrance comes from no earlier than 1824, but still well within reach of the seasonal encampments still occurring in 1817.

"Old Hungry"

According to Margaret Thacher Drury's *Scrapbook*, Elbridge Marshall's daughter, Faustina, remembered as a girl an Indian who came to their house in the New Town area looking for food. He had been given the unflattering nickname of "Old Hungry," and these visits to the Marshall farm at what is now 455 Newtown Road occurred between when Faustina was born in 1850 and when she married Albert O. Lawrence in 1874.

Indian visits to the Marshall farm had been an ongoing tradition from at least Elbridge's childhood to his daughter Fustina's childhood. Another home in the New Town area with a tradition of Indian visits was the Whitney-Hoar house.

The visits to the Marshall home in the 1860s era are the last recorded "Nashobah Indian" sightings in Littleton. Perhaps it is better put that these were the last sightings in Littleton where Indians looked and acted "Indian," and as such were cause for comment.

The Last Indian?

In the wake of King Philip's War and the disintegration of the Eliot-style Praying villages, some Native elements resurfaced and by and large they created "a new Indian identity," according to Mandell, which rather than being a clash of culture became "neither English nor Algonquin, but a combination of the two," weighted more heavily toward the Indian. They lived their own way now and it was a blend, but it was of their own making. They even adopted the English concept of land ownership.

In Natick, where most of the Praying Indians ended up after King Philip's War, including the Nashobah, they attended services in an English meetinghouse, but were led by a Native preacher. They organized their town into English-style house lots, but many still lived in wigwams.

The Praying Indians reverted back to being led by sachems with successionship, not appointments, and relied on clan boundaries as the primary form of social organization, according to Jill

Lepore in *The Name of War*, 1998. These were no longer Eliot-led Praying villages, but a new and adaptive form of Indian social structure under their own control. By doing so, they managed to preserve much of their traditional culture.

Note 18: Mandell echoes this in Behind the Frontier and elaborates: "Aboriginal leadership patterns reemerged after resettlement, in part from the Indian's needs and desires, and in part because provincial officials (and their legal systems) found Sagamores, Sachems, and their heirs useful in obtaining land in the region."

In the years that followed King Philip's War, even up to Harwood's time, the Nashobah Indians did not disappear. Rather, they became increasingly integrated into Colonial and American society. They didn't vanish in some nineteenth-century haze of romanticism, but instead became near invisible as a culture—but not as people. They are still here today.

AFTERWORD

Return of the Nashobah
With message from Chief Caring Hands

I had the good fortune of growing up in Littleton and spent much of my boyhood camping and fishing in the Nagog Pond area; I knew the Jenkins-Knapp (Sarah Doublet Forest) property well. I knew that the Indians had lived here under Chief Tahattawan long ago, and although I didn't know much more than that, I had a youthful sense that the area of Fort Pond Hill and Nagog Pond was sacred land.

Later in life I continued to be drawn here, to its sense of the sacred, and after moving back to town as an adult I spent a good 20 years walking this land as a researcher, historian, and witness of its spirit, writing and giving talks on Nashobah.

What I wanted people to know was simple—that Littleton was on sacred land and the heart of it was the hill between Nagog and Fort ponds. It was—*is*—a scared place of shaman and vision-quest, and a place where the Nashobah Praying Indians worshipped Creator and praised *Manit Wame Nasugkenuk*, which means God Almighty, as translated by Rev. Eliot in the Massachusett Natick Bible.

There were times I felt I walked in two worlds—a foot in the present, and a foot in Nashobah times.

I lamented the fact that the Nashobah were long gone. Sometimes I felt I could feel their spirit, but mostly I felt it slumbered a long deep sleep beneath the hill. I had no power to wake it.

Strong Bear Medicine

Life has many surprises. Late in the autumn of 2017, Ann Himmelberger of the Littleton Historical Society attended a program in Westford about the discovery of the Grassy Pond stone circle and had the good fortune to meet Chief Black Eagle and Strong Bear Medicine. When Ann introduced herself as being from Littleton, Strong Bear Medicine recognized the town and replied that he was a Nashobah of Chief Tahattawan's people and was a Praying Indian.

Ann summed it up for us all when she recounted later, "You could have knocked me over with a feather. I never expected I would ever meet someone who claimed ancestry from the Nashobah group. There they were—looking just as I would hope and expect Tahattawan's ancestors might look."

From this unexpected encounter a long and abiding friendship arose between the Nashobah and members of the Littleton Historical Society, and Littleton Conservation Trust.

So where had they been all this time? "We've always been here," Strong Bear told me, "but no one thinks to look." He is correct; it never occurred to me to google the tribe.

AFTERWORD

The Nashobah Today

I am pleased to say that the Nashobah—the Nashobah-Natick-Ponkapoag Praying Indians to be exact—are alive and well under the guidance of their chief, Chief Caring Hands.

There were many historical ties between Nashobah and Natick Praying Villages, and after King Philip's War, most of the Nashobah relocated to Natick. As related on the Natick Praying Indian website:

"In the aftermath of the King Philip's War, and nearly eliminated through the devastation of Deer Island, the Massachusett Natick Praying Indian people maintained a presence in Natick. They welcomed others dispossessed of their praying Indian Villages. The Indian Church, Peletiah's Tavern (Peletiah's Tavern, Natick, MA), the Indian burial grounds (within Natick, MA) Lake Cochituate (Wayland/Natick) and Waban remained central to the existing Natick Indian community and to the ancestral memory of the indigenous people of God."

As for Natick and Rev. Eliot, the Praying Indians say this:

"In 1651 by order of the Massachusetts General Court, Natick was established as the first praying Indian village/town. The place was set apart for Waban and the Praying Indians so that Waban's Massachusett people could worship in peace unmolested by the colonists and the surrounding disagreeable Native tribes. In the beginning there were 51 inhabitants of the Natick Praying Indian Village which would be the first Christian town in the country. Natick means 'Place of Searching' though often referred to as the 'Place of Many Hills' or 'My Home.' Natick is the 'Mother Village' of the seven original or 'Old Praying Towns' and the seven villages that would follow for a total of 14 Praying Indian Towns.

The Reverend John Eliot was loved by the new Christian native people and became known to all men as the 'Apostle to the Indians.' Natick is home of the first Praying Indian Church (present day Eliot Church of South Natick, MA). It was the only church to call its members to prayer service by its drum."

In fact, it still does. The Natick Praying Indians resumed worship service more than 300 years later at the South Natick Eliot Church, on the very spot where they originally worshipped with Rev. Eliot in a clearing marked by four oak trees. On August 11, 2012, the heartbeat of the drum was heard again in this sacred place, and it continues to be heard every second Saturday of the month.

It has been my privilege to attend their monthly public worship service presided over by Chief Caring Hands, with Still Water, Quiet Storm, Strong Bull, Strong Bear Medicine, and many others. As well, together we have made many walkabouts with the Chief's family in their ancestral lands of Nashobah. The spirit that slumbered under the hill has awoken.

It is my pleasure to see the Nashobah visible in Littleton again, taking their rightful place in the community and offering their prayers to the Creator on the hill by the pond.

Tahattawan's people have returned.

MESSAGE FROM CHIEF CARING HANDS

"Although we are not the only descendants, we are the only existing Praying Indian Tribe. The blood of a praying Indian is both physical and spiritual. Our lineage of both is unbroken. We have seen our brothers and sisters, descendants of shared heritage deviate from the path and acknowledge the weight of an overwhelming history. In suffering the loss of family and brethren we recognize the difficulty of the walk of our praying Indian ancestors. We have understood that boundaries are spiritual as well as physical. Shunned for years by the Native community, we are rewarded in now witnessing resurgence of our praying Indian brethren.

As the earth reclines under the grass, so too does the earth recline under the Great Spirit of God. Therefore the chosen habitations thereof are a principle of God understood by all indigenous people (moskhet kutoo). We are mindful of our past, of all our native brothers and sisters suffering and the wish of all non-natives of good hearts to reconcile. This can be done only through the people wronged, forgotten and holding out the scepter of reconciliation. True restoration is more than a word. As a chief honored in the spiritual lineage of Waban, first indigenous minister of light and a remnant surviving the physical and spiritual holocaust of a blessed people, the Praying Indians stand as first ambassadors of this country to the world. In an inordinate display of reconciliation we extend our hand to our captors. As we hold out the scepter understand that restoration is more than a word.

I am proud to be Chief of the Mother Village of all Praying Indians. I am proud of the tribe which has stood by my leadership and against the tide of suffering and misunderstanding. We do not apologize for our belief in love of The Father God and His Son First Spoken Word of Light. Even those who do not agree must honor the strength of standing for one's beliefs. As a chief watching her people suffer the isolation of a social Deer Island, I see as Waban saw in facing his people on Deer Island. Waban, can you see me? In an echo from the past do we stand alongside all our ancestors and welcome our brethren in the name of Word Faithful and True. We are who we are. We stand where we stand. We are the Massachusett Praying Indians. In thoughts ever toward peace I say A'ho. I have spoken. I am Naticksqw Chief Caring Hands, she who speaks for her people."

A'ho!

- Chief Caring Hands

APPENDIX

The aptly named Job Kattenanit was a Praying Indian minister from Natick. He had been at Hassanamesit when it was captured by Nipmuck warriors, and the 200 Praying Indians there had been persuaded to go with them, many willingly, and join Metacom. Captain Tom was one of the Indians who went willingly. Among the unwilling was Joseph Tukapewillin, the minster of the Hassanamesit church. James Speen was there as well, and both Job and James escaped, but in doing so, Job left his three children with the Nipmuck.

Job was able to get a safe conduct pass from Gookin in his bid to rescue his children. There is no mention of his wife in any of the accounts, and it is assumed he was a widower. But before he could rescue his children, he was caught by the English, who disregarded his pass, and was sent to prison in Boston and then to Deer Island. Here Gookin found him in December of 1675, when he was looking for Praying Indians to spy on the Nipmuck.

Job was engaged and sent out, and while on his mission met up with Joseph Tukapewillin. Together they devised a plan to rescue their families and rejoin the English. Before Job left to bring word to the English of the impending attack on Lancaster, he set up a safe rendezvous location near Hassanamesit for his friends and family where he would meet them on his return and take them to safety with the English.

Unfortunately, after giving his intelligence to the English he was put right back on Deer Island, and was unable to rescue his family. However, in late February, six more Praying Indians were recruited off the island as scouts for Major Savage after it was learned that "the Indians were in three Towns beyond Quaboge." Among those granted release from the island was Job Kattenanit.

When Savage got near Marlborough, Job got leave to search for his children, who were still waiting at the meeting place but were low on food. Tukapewillin and his family were there as well, including his 80-year-old father. There was also a widow and her daughter with them. The widow had carefully kept and fed Job's children from when they were first forced to go with the Nipmuck.

Upon their return, they were caught by a party of English, who took all their possessions and abused them to the point that both Tukapewillin's wife and the widow ran off into the woods for fear of being murdered. Tukapewillin's 13-year-old son and the widow's daughter ran with them, and Tukapewillin's wife left behind her three-month-old baby.

When they were finally turned over to Major Savage, both Job and Joseph and their remaining children were sent to Deer Island, where a nurse was found for the baby. A week or so after that, Tom Dublet found the women and children and brought them in, but sadly, Joseph's son had died of exposure. From there they were sent to Deer Island, and reunited with Job and James.

As related by Gookin, after the many hardships, the years that followed were kind to Job. "This widow Job married afterward, not knowing how better to requite her love showed in nourishing and preferring his three children when they were among the enemies, and they now lived comfortably together; so that after all the troubles, sorrows, and calamities this man Job underwent, God gave him all his children in safety, and a suitable wife; and vindicated him from all the calumnies and aspersions cast on him, and by good demonstrations cleared his integrity and faithfulness to God's cause and the English interest, and hath made him very serviceable and victorious since, in the war against the enemy."

BIBLIOGRAPHY

Acton Historical Society, *A Brief History of the Town of Acton*, 1974

Barry, William, *A History of Framingham, Massachusetts, Including the Plantation, From 1640 to the Present Time*, 1847

Beals, Charles Edward Jr., *Passaconaway in the White Mountains*, 1916

Bodge, George Madison, *Soldiers in King Philip's War*, 1906

Bonfanti, Leo, *New England Indians* Vol. I, 1968

Bowers, Andrew T., *Conversation with Daniel V. Boudillion*, 1997

Bowers, Andrew T., *Conversation with Daniel V. Boudillion*, 2000

Brodeur, Paul, *Peaceful Indians Forced to Scatter*, Main Street Journal, Marlborough, December 12, 2016

Butterworth, Hezekiah, *Popular History of Boston*, 1893

Butterworth, Hezekiah, *Young Folk's History of Boston*, 1881

Cannole, Dennis A., *The Indians of the Nipmuck Country in Southern New England 1630-1750: An Historical Geography*, 2001

Cobbet, the Rev. Thomas, *A Narrative of New England Deliverances*, 1677

Cody, David, *Puritanism in New England*, 1988

Cogley, Richard W., *John Eliot's Mission to the Indians before King Philip's War*, 1999

Currier, John, *How Neshobe Came Up Into the Green Mountains; Also the Discovery of Lake Bombazon by Samuel de Champlain*, 1914

Daniels, George Fisher, *The Huguenots in the Nipmuck Country or Oxford Prior to 1713*, 1880

Daunton, Martin & Halpern, Rick, *Empire and Others: British Encounters with Indigenous Peoples 1600-1850*, 1999

Davison, Ken, *Mohegan Archaeological Field School Enters Third Week*, Feather News, July 8, 2009

Drake, Samuel Gardner, *Book of the Indians*, 1845

Drake, Samuel Gardner, *History of the Early Discovery of America and the Landing of the Pilgrims: with a Biography of the North American Indians*, 1854

Drake, Samuel Gardner, *Old Indian Chronicle*, Annotated Edition, 1867

Drake, Samuel Gardner, *The Aboriginal Races of North America*, 1859

Drake, Samuel Gardner, *The New England Historical & Genealogical Register, Volume I.*, 1847

Drury, Margaret Thacher, *Margaret Drury's Scrapbook*, Littleton Historical Society *

Egerton, John, *Nashoba*, Tennessee Encyclopedia of History and Culture, 1998

Eliot, John, *A Brief Narrative of the Progress of the Gospel Amongst the Indians in New England, In the Year 1670: A letter to the Commissioners for the Propagation of the Gospel*, 1670

Eliot, John, *Up-Biblum God*, 1663

Ellis, George W., and Morris, John E. *King Philip's War*, 1906

Emerson, Wilimena H., *Genealogy of the Descendants of John Eliot, "Apostle to the Indians" 1598-1905* 1905

Fairfield, Oliver Jay, *The Town of Littleton Massachusetts, Past and Present*, 1914 **

Fletcher, Rev. James, *Acton in History*, 1890

Frost, Edward, *Littleton Historical Society, Proceedings No. 1, 1894-1895*, 1896 *

Frothingham, Richard Jr., *The History of Charlestown, Massachusetts*, 1856

Gage, James, *Email correspondence with Daniel V. Boudillion*, January 2020

Gookin, Daniel, *Doings and Sufferings of the Christian Indians in New England in the Years 1675-1677*, 1677

Gookin, Daniel, *Historical Collections of the Indians in New England*, 1674

Green, Samuel, A., *Groton During the Indian Wars*, 1883

Harwood, Herbert J., *Historical Sketch of Littleton*, 1890 *

Harwood, Herbert J., *Littleton Historical Society, Proceedings no. 1, 1894-1895*, 1896 *

Hubbard, William, *Narrative of the Indian Wars in New-England*, 1677

Huden, John C., *Indian Place Names of New England*, 1962

Hudson, Alfred Sereno, *The History of Concord, Massachusetts, Volume I, Colonial Concord*, 1904

Hudson, Alfred Sereno, *The History of Sudbury, Massachusetts, 1638-1889*, 1889

Hutchinson, Thomas, *History of Massachusetts*, 1795

Knight, Ellen, *The Sachems of the Massachusetts Bay*, 2018

Lechford, Thomas, *Plaine Dealing, or Newes from New England*, 1642

Lepore, Jill, *The Name of War: King Philip's War and the Origins of American Identity*, 1998

Lepore, Jill, *When Deer Island Was Turned Into Devils Island*, Bostonia magazine, summer 1998

Levinson, Betsy, "We are still here" say Nipmucks of southeastern Mass., Littleton Independent, September 10, 2009

Littleton Bicentennial Commission, *Town of Littleton*, 1975 **

MacCulloch, Susan L., *A Tripartite Political System among Christian Indians of Early Massachusetts*, Kroeber Anthropological Society Papers 34 (1966): 63–73

Mandell, Daniel R., *Behind the Frontier: Indians in Eighteenth-Century Massachusetts*, 1996

Marchione, Dr. William P., *John Eliot and Nonantum*, Allston-Brighton Tab, July of 1998

Massachusetts General Court, House of Representatives, *Report of the Joint Special Committee Upon the Subject of the Flowage of Meadows on Concord and Sudbury Rivers*, 1860

Massachusetts Historical Commission, *Inventory of Historic Homes, 511 Newtown Road, Littleton, Mass.*, 1998 *

Mavor, James W. Jr., and Dix, Byron E., *Manitou: The Sacred Landscape of New England's Native Civilization*, 1989

Mitchell, John Hanson, *Trespassing*, 1998

Morison, Samuel Eliot, *Historical Markers Erected by Massachusetts Bay Colony Tercentenary Commission*, 1930

Nipmuck Association of Connecticut, *Historical Series Number 3*, 1995

Palfrey, John Gorham, *History of New England volume III*, 1892

Phalen, Harold R., *History of the Town of Acton*, 1954

Philbrick, Nathaniel, *Mayflower: A Story of Courage, Community, and War*, 2006

Powell, Summer Chilton, *Puritan Village: The Foundation of a New England Town*, 1963

Prendergast, John, *The Cromwellian Settlement of Ireland*, 1870

Proctor, Joel, *Information of Joel Proctor Aged 89 Years*, April 19, 1894, Collection Littleton Historical Society *

Sanderson, George A., *Littleton Historical Society, Proceedings No. 1, 1894-1895*, 1896 *

Savage, James, *A Genealogical Dictionary of the First Settlers of New England, Showing Three Generations of those who came before May, 1692, on the basis of Farmer's Register*, 1860-62

Seeman, Erik R., *Death in the New World: Cross-Cultural Encounters, 1492-1800*, 2010

Sewell, Samuel, *Diary*, 1674-1729

Shattuck, Lemuel, *A History of the Town of Concord; Middlesex County, Massachusetts, From its Earliest Settlement to 1832*, 1835

Sheppard, Thomas, *The Clear Sunshine of the Gospel, Breaking Forth Upon the Indians in New-England*, 1648.

Swanton, John, *Indian Tribes of North America*, 1953.

Temple, J. H., *History of Framingham, Massachusetts, Early Known as Danforth's Farms, 1640-1880*, 1887

Thompson, Daniel, *Green Mountain Boys*, 1839

Tooker, William Wallace, *American Anthropologist*, September, 1897

Tooker, William Wallace, *The Significance of the John Eliot's Natick and the Name Merrimac*, 1901

Trumbull, J. Hammond, *The Composition of Indian Geographical Names*, 1870

Trumbull, J. Hammond, *Natick Dictionary*, 1903

Wiser, Ron, *Ron Wiser Research Home Page*, July 2000

Walcott, Charles H., *Concord in the Colonial Period*, 1884

Waters, Henry Fritz-Gilbert, *New England Historical and Genealogical Register*, Vol. VII, Pages 209-219, New England Historic Genealogical Society, 1853

Webster, Carolyn, *Phenomena of the Elements*, Littleton Legends, Turner's Public Spirit (Ayer, Massachusetts), May 9, 1957 *

Weeks, Daniel J., *Not for Filthy Lucre's Sake: Richard Saltar and the Antiproprietary Movement in East New Jersey, 1665-1707*, 2001

Winsor, Justin in the 1880 *Memorial History of Boston: Including Suffolk County, Massachusetts 1630-1880*, 1880

Websites:

Boyer, Paul, *Apocalypticism Explained: The Puritans*, PBS/Frontline:

http://www.pbs.org/wgbh/pages/frontline/shows/apocalypse/explanation/puritans.html

Braintree Historical Society, https://sites.google.com/site/thebraintreehistoricalsociety/home

History of the New England Company, www.newenglandcompany.org, 2004

Indian vs. English Views Regarding Rights to the Land, Southern Essex District Registry of Deeds, www.salemdeeds.com

New England Company, http://www.newenglandcompany.org

Massachusett Tribe at Ponkapoag, http://massachusetttribe.org

Museum of the American Indian, www.nmai.si.edu

Praying Indians of Natick and Ponkapoag, http://natickprayingindians.org

Winchester, Town of, *The Sachems of the Massachusetts Bay*, no date given www.winchester.us

Wiser, Ron, *Ron Wiser Research Home Page*, July 2000 Freepages.geanealogy.rootsweb.ancestory.com

Maps:

Beers, F. W., *Atlas of Middlesex County, Massachusetts*, 1875

Hoar & Foster, *Plan of Littleton*, 1830 *

Smith, Paul E, *Massachusetts State Department of Agriculture, Map of Littleton*, 1932, revised by Paul Smith 1957 *

Smith, Samuel, *Smith Plat*, Littleton Historical Society, circa 1879 *

USGS, *Lowell Quadrangle*, 1893, 15-minute series, surveyed 1886

USGS, *Westford Quadrangle*, 1941, 7.5 minute series, surveyed 1939

Walling, Henry Francis, *Atlas of Middlesex County, Massachusetts*, 1856

Archives:

Ancient Records of Concord, Vol. 1, Page 160

County Court Files, 1668, 1675

First Church Records, Roxbury

James Quanapaug's Information, *Collections of the Massachusetts Historical Society*, VI. 205-208

Massachusetts Colony Records, Vol. 5, Page 83, also Pages 93, 94

Massachusetts Records, Vol 1, Page 196

Massachusetts Archives, Vol. 30, Page 81

Massachusetts Archives, Vol. 30, Page 183

Massachusetts Archives, Vol. 30, Page 185a

Massachusetts Archives, Vol. 30, Page 186-7

Massachusetts Archives, Vol. 30, Page 189a

Massachusetts Archives, Vol. 30, Page 190

Massachusetts Archives, Vol. 30, Page 197

Massachusetts Archives, Vol. 30, Page 199

Massachusetts Archives, Vol. 30, Page 200a

Massachusetts Archives, Vol. 30, Page 201b

Massachusetts Archives, Vol. 30, Page 203a

Massachusetts Archives, Vol. 30, Page 207

Massachusetts Archives, Vol. 30, Page 258a

Massachusetts Archives, Vol. 30, Page 261

Massachusetts Archives, Vol. 30, Page 279

Massachusetts Archives, Vol. 30, Page 305

Massachusetts Archives Vol. 30, Pages 348-9

Massachusetts Archives, Vol. 30, Pages 474-5

Massachusetts Archives, Vol. 30, Page 486

Massachusetts Archives, Vol. 30, Page 488

Massachusetts Archives, Vol. 30, Page 489

Massachusetts Archives, Vol. 30, Page 493b

Massachusetts Archives, Vol. 31, Page 391

Massachusetts Archives, Vol. 113, Page 193

Massachusetts Archives, Vol. 113, Page 330

Massachusetts Archives, Vol. 113, Page 603

Massachusetts Registry of Deeds, Book 45, Page 477

Middlesex Deeds, Lib. 9, Fol. 105

Records of the Colony of New Plymouth of New England, Vol. I., 1633-1640

Southern Middlesex Registry of Deeds, Vol. 9, Page 106

* May be found at the Littleton Historical Society
** May be found at the Reuben Hoar Library, Littleton

ABOUT THE AUTHOR

Daniel V. Boudillion is an avid historian with a wide knowledge of early Nashobah-Littleton history and the locations associated with them. He grew up in Littleton, Massachusetts and explored the Nashobah lands since he was a young boy, locating many lost historical sites in the area.

He is currently on the board of the Littleton Historical Society, a Trustee of the Littleton Conservation Trust, on the Steering Committee of Friends of Pine Hawk, founder of Nashobah CSL, founder of the Friends of the Nashobah Praying Indians, and was previously webmaster for New England Antiquities Research Association. He has given numerous talks and walks in the area on Littleton-Nashobah history and is a featured speaker. His work has been featured the *NEARA Journal* and *Weird Massachusetts*.

He resides in Littleton with his wife Julie and their daughter Caitlin.

www.ingramcontent.com/pod-product-compliance
Lightning Source LLC
Chambersburg PA
CBHW070538090426
42735CB00013B/3019